Witnessing to the Kingdom: Melbourne and Beyond

Edited by
GERALD H. ANDERSON

ORBIS BOOKS

Maryknoll, New York 10545

BV
2070
.W57
1982

The Catholic Foreign Mission Society of America (Maryknoll) recruits and trains people for overseas missionary service. Through Orbis Books Maryknoll aims to foster the international dialogue that is essential to mission. The books published, however, reflect the opinions of their authors and are not meant to represent the official position of the society.

Manuscript editor: Lisa McGaw

Library of Congress Cataloging in Publication Data
Main entry under title:

Witnessing to the kingdom.

  Bibliography: p.
  1. Missions—Addresses, essays, lectures.
2. Kingdom of God—Addresses, essays, lectures.
3. World Conference on Mission and Evangelism
(1980: Melbourne, Vic.)—Addresses, essays, lectures.   I. Anderson Gerald H.
BV2070.W57   266   82-3530
ISBN 0-88344-708-8 (pbk.)   AACR2

The prayer for a coming kingdom is a prayer of responsibility. It challenges us to give ourselves in service to the God for whose kingdom we pray, not counting the cost but pledging all. Our mission is to proclaim the Word of God, to name the Name of Jesus Christ, that all humanity may respond to the call our Lord presents, and turn to him. Our mission is also to offer good news to the poor, to heal the sick, to proclaim liberty to the captive, to provide sight to the blind, to announce the acceptable time of the Lord.

From "Litany of the Kingdom," used in worship at the Melbourne Conference

Contents

Foreword

EMILIO CASTRO

More than a year has passed since the Melbourne Conference, but memories are still very vivid: Of Ernst Käsemann, like an Old Testament prophet, calling Christianity to become a movement of resistance to the manipulative forces of the anti-kingdom, and to have the courage to announce a kingdom that breaks through all oppressive realities and calls for an entirely new reality. . . . Of Julia Esquivel describing God's pain in the suffering and struggle of the peasants of Guatemala, or of Metropolitan Osthathios pleading for a gospel that fully manifests the total abasement of the Son of God and his identification with the poor of the earth.

Above all, the memories that remain are those of a prayerful and worshiping encounter. Who could forget the frequent singing of "Jesus, remember me when you come into your kingdom," or "Your kingdom come, O Lord, your kingdom come, O Lord." But, of course, these memories are limited to the privileged group of delegates who had a chance to participate in this significant event. The report of the conference has been published here to share with many others the results of two weeks of intensive discussion, wrestling, and praying together. They give testimony to the common convictions prevailing in Melbourne, but surely they are not the final word; they have paved the way for practical implementation and for deeper reflection in areas of missionary action that Melbourne could not tackle in its totality.

It is, therefore, very appropriate that this book should be published in the United States with the double intention to indicate how the main issues of the Melbourne Conference speak to the North American scene, and to indicate from the North American perspective the issues that remain to be tackled, problems to be confronted, challenges to be raised. We trust that the implications of Melbourne will be suggested for our readers outside North America as well. If this is a book that springs from the participation in the World Conference on Mission and Evangelism, held in Melbourne in May 1980, it is a book not bound to yesterday, but looking at the realities of today and the promises of the future. What does it mean to accept good news to the poor as the commanding missiological principle for our missionary obedience today? How do we develop a style of mission that will help to make our mission credible in the eyes of the poor of the earth? There is a frank discussion of the potentialities and the difficulties facing local congregations in their attempt to live up to the challenges of the kingdom. Melbourne was in itself a microcosm of the Christian church, an ecumenical meeting in the widest sense of the word, both involving delegates coming from churches of old Christian traditions and persuasions and also bringing Christians from entirely different contexts, so that the dialogue about our missionary obedience was fed not only from classical confessions and their theological position, but also from the diversity of conflicting situations in the world where Christians are trying to be faithful to their missionary calling. This book will help the readers not only to understand the Orthodox theology and practice of mission, but also to discern the importance of their contribution to the findings of the Melbourne Conference. The Roman Catholic position is stated with clarity and, paradoxically, is a help and calling to overcome dichotomies inside the Protestant camp. We are challenged also to reaffirm the missionary calling of all Christian churches, considering the fact that the majority of the poor of the earth are those who are deprived of the knowledge of Jesus Christ.

Melbourne made two fundamental affirmations that are normally held in opposition, but there they were brought into a constructive dialectic: the gospel is announced to the poor, and in order to do so, Christians and churches must be involved in all the struggles of history. The center of the mission of the church, the paradigm of the kingdom, is the celebration of the Holy Communion, bread for missionaries. Activism and contemplation are the depth of our faith and the outpouring of our missionary love—these two sources of missionary zeal permeated the Melbourne Conference and are very much present in concrete forms in the pages of this book.

Introduction

GERALD H. ANDERSON

In Melbourne, Australia, May 12–24, 1980, the Commission on World Mission and Evangelism of the World Council of Churches (CWME/WCC) convened a World Conference on Mission and Evangelism. This was the ninth in a series of world missionary conferences, beginning with the Edinburgh Conference of 1910, that Philip Potter describes as "a long pilgrimage, from Edinburgh to Melbourne."

Over six hundred participants—Orthodox, Roman Catholic, and Protestant—from one hundred countries, came to Melbourne in response to an invitation "to join in a process of prayer, reflection, search and obedience under the conference theme 'Your Kingdom Come.' " The expectation of CWME for the Melbourne Conference was expressed in preconference materials: "We hope for fresh insights, for answers to urgent questions which come from prayer and reflection on the kingdom in specific missionary situations." Emilio Castro, the CWME director, said that the purpose of the conference was "to re-think the missionary and evangelical vocation of the church. Our aim is to help churches in fulfilling their missionary vocation."

Meeting on the campus of Melbourne University and using five official languages in their deliberations, participants spent fourteen hours during the conference in small groups for Bible study, where they shared their reflections on the meaning of the Lord's Prayer as found in Matthew's Gospel. They also met in sections and plenary sessions to think and pray together, under the discipline of God's Word, about the following themes important for the task of mission and evangelism today: I. Good News to the Poor; II. The Kingdom of God and Human Struggles; III. The Church Witnesses to the Kingdom; IV. Christ—Crucified and

Risen—Challenges Human Power. The reports from these sections, as amended and adopted by the conference, are included in the appendix of this volume.

In many ways the Melbourne Conference was a healing and pastoral experience for those involved in the world mission of the church. In contrast to the confrontation and polarization in much discussion about the Christian mission in recent years, there was considerable convergence among participants at Melbourne about the crucial issues that measure our faithfulness and test our effectiveness in mission today.

The focus at Melbourne was on "the poor" in relation to the kingdom. While there were differences of interpretation about the meaning and implications of this emphasis, the report of Section I, for instance, on "Good News to the Poor" declares that "in the perspective of the kingdom, God has a preference for the poor." And it urged that "churches will need to surrender their attitudes of benevolence and charity by which they have condescended to the poor; in many cases this will mean a radical change in the institutional life of the missionary movement." In his foreword to this volume, Emilio Castro speaks of "good news to the poor as the commanding missiological principle for our missionary obedience today." Elsewhere Castro has observed that at Melbourne "the relation to the poor . . . is the criterion to judge the authenticity and credibility of the Church's missionary engagement. . . . The missiological principle, the missionary yardstick, is the relation of the Church to the poor." Perhaps this point, more than any other, is the abiding contribution of Melbourne toward an understanding of the Christian mission for our time.

Melbourne was concerned with world evangelization. The theme of the kingdom of God is an evangelistic theme. Several times during the conference it was pointed out that the great majority of the world's population that has not been reached with the gospel happens also to be largely the poor of the earth. Therefore the final message of the assembly to the churches declares both that "we . . . are challenged by the suffering of the poor," and "we pray that they may hear the gospel." This affirms the announcement of Jesus at the beginning of his ministry—quoting from the prophet Isaiah—"The spirit of the Lord is upon me,

because he has anointed me to preach good news to the poor. . ."
(Lk. 4:18). Section II, 23, stated that "the proclamation of the
Gospel to the whole world remains an urgent obligation for all
Christians," and Section III, 7, acknowledged "our special obligation to those who have never heard the Good News of the
kingdom." The understanding of evangelism, however, is always
"holistic," witnessing to the whole gospel of the kingdom (cf.
Mk. 1:14), including both word and deed. Indeed, "the credibility
of the proclamation of the Word of God rests upon the authenticity of the total witness of the church" (Section III, 6).

The missionary and evangelistic nature of the Melbourne Conference, however, is not to be found primarily in its statements
about the mandate for world evangelization. Rather, it is in the
challenge and commitment that permeated the conference, calling for the total liberation/redemption of all human beings, and
requiring a style of missionary witness that is profoundly contextual and incarnational.

In a sense it would be fair to say that Melbourne was not a
traditional missionary conference, precisely because the church is
no longer in a traditional missionary situation. Melbourne discerned "a change in the direction of mission, arising from our
understanding of the Christ who is the center and who is always in
movement towards the periphery. . . . This development, we expect, will take the form of ever stronger initiatives from the
churches of the poor and oppressed at peripheries" (Section IV,
24).

To all those who rejoice in what God is doing in his world and
with his church, Melbourne offers a contemporary statement on
mission and evangelism that suggests new and hopeful possibilities for witnessing to the kingdom. In this volume we have asked
several persons from the United States who participated in the
Melbourne Conference to share their impressions and reactions,
especially in terms of implications for the churches in North
America. We urge the members of our churches to hear and share
the message from the conference to the churches, especially when
it states: "In the name of Jesus Christ we have come. Our attention focused on the prayer Jesus taught us: 'Your Kingdom come.'
This prayer disturbs us and comforts us, yet by it we are united."

Litany of Thanksgiving:
Edinburgh 1910 to Melbourne 1980*

LEADER: (Edinburgh, 1910) O Lord, we give you thanks for those who opened the modern ecumenical era by coming together in Edinburgh. We are grateful for the passion they had to communicate the gospel to every creature.

RESPONSE: *Keep us together, Lord, and rekindle among us such a vision for our day.*

LEADER: (Jerusalem, 1928) O Lord, we give you thanks for those who went back to Jerusalem and to the sources of our faith, committing themselves to renewal in mission. We are grateful for their courage in facing the realities of a growing technological and industrial world and in defining mission in ways relevant to that new reality.

RESPONSE: *Lord, grant us the same roots in your Word and the same courage to open ourselves to the realities of our time.*

LEADER: (Tambaram, India, 1938) O Lord, we give you thanks for those who in Tambaram discovered the church as the active bearer of the gospel. We are grateful for their honest attempt to give witness to the uniqueness of Jesus Christ in a world of universal religions.

*From a service of worship at the Melbourne Conference.

RESPONSE: *Lord, help us and our churches to discern signs of your kingdom among all cultures and peoples. Help us to give humble witness to our own experience in Christ.*

LEADER: (Whitby, Canada, 1947) Lord, we give thanks for the recognition at Whitby of churches as partners in obedience to a common missionary calling. We thank you for their readiness to participate in the reconstruction of a world ravaged by war.

RESPONSE: *Lord, help us to realize more fully the meaning of our partnership, and the peculiar tasks that are ours in the permanent reconstruction of a world ravaged by hate and destruction.*

LEADER: (Willingen, Federal Republic of Germany, 1952) We worship you, O God, as the missionary God who through your creating, judging, and redeeming action are bringing all things to a final uniting in Christ; and we thank you for the fellowship we enjoy with you and with one another through participation in your mission.

RESPONSE: *Help us, Lord, through the vision of your kingdom to be present with you in your work.*

LEADER: (Achimota, Ghana, 1957-58) We thank you, O Lord, for the integration of the International Missionary Council into the World Council of Churches. We thank you for the vision of a church united in mission.

RESPONSE: *Grant, O Lord, that the work we do here may enhance the fulfillment of that vision.*

LEADER: (Mexico City, 1963) We thank you, Lord, for the coming together of Orthodox, Roman Catholic, and Protestant Christians in a common search for

missionary obedience. We thank you for the awareness of missionary challenges in every continent.

RESPONSE: *Help us to bring forth the fruits of that diversity in
unity for the evangelization of all the continents.*

LEADER: (Bangkok, 1972–73) We thank you, O Lord, for the
reality of your salvation manifest in every culture.
We thank you for your good news of salvation that
sends us in your name into the social, political, and
cultural struggles of the world.

RESPONSE: *Grant us faithfulness to respond to the grace of
your salvation.*

Message to the Churches
from the Melbourne Conference
on World Mission and Evangelism

Dear Sisters and Brothers in Christ:

We, more than five hundred Christians from many of the world's nations, have gathered in Melbourne, Australia, May 12-24, 1980, in the World Council of Churches' Conference on World Mission and Evangelism. In the name of Jesus Christ we have come. Our attention focused on the prayer Jesus taught us: "Your Kingdom come." This prayer disturbs us and comforts us, yet by it we are united.

We meet under the clouds of nuclear threat and annihilation. Our world is deeply wounded by the oppressions inflicted by the powerful on the powerless. These oppressions are found in our economic, political, racial, sexual and religious life. Our world, so proud of human achievements, is full of people suffering from hunger, poverty and injustice. People are wasted.

> Have they no knowledge, all the evildoers who eat up my people as they eat bread? (Psalm 14:4)

The poor and the hungry cry to God. Our prayer "Your kingdom come" must be prayed in solidarity with the cry of millions who are living in poverty and injustice. Peoples suffer the pain of silent torment; their faces reveal their suffering. The church cannot live distant from these faces because she sees the face of Jesus in them (Matthew 25).

In such a world the announcement of the kingdom of God comes to all. It comes to the poor and in them generates the power to affirm their human dignity, liberation and hope. To the oppressor it comes as judgement, challenge and a call for repentance. To the insensitive it comes as a call to awareness of responsibility. The church itself has often failed its Lord by hindering the coming of his kingdom. We admit this sin and our need for repentance, forgiveness and cleansing.

The Triune God, revealed in the person and work of Jesus Christ, is the center of all peoples and all things. Our Savior Jesus Christ was laid in a manger "because there was no place for him in the inn" (Luke 2:7). He is central to life, yet moves toward those on the edge of life. He affirms his lordship by giving it up. He was crucified "outside the gate" (Hebrews 13:12). In this surrender of power he establishes his power to heal. The good news of the kingdom must be presented to the world by the church, the Body of Christ, the sacrament of the kingdom in every place and time. It is through the Holy Spirit that the kingdom is brought to its final consummation.

People who suffer injustice are on the periphery of national and community life. Multitudes are economically and politically oppressed. Often these are the people who have not heard of the Gospel of Jesus Christ. But Jesus Christ comes to them. He exercises his healing authority on the periphery. We, participants in this Conference on World Mission and Evangelism, are challenged by the suffering of the poor. We pray that they may hear the Gospel and that all of us may be worthy proclaimers of the Gospel by word and life. We stand under the judgement and the hope of Jesus Christ. The prayer "Your kingdom come" brings us closer to Jesus Christ in today's world. We invite you to join us in commitment to the Lord for the coming of whose kingdom we pray.

Your kingdom come, O Lord.

From Edinburgh to Melbourne*

PHILIP POTTER

The World Council of Churches is proud to be the inheritor of the great missionary movement that launched the decisive stage of the ecumenical movement at Edinburgh 1910. It was therefore natural that when the World Council was formed in 1948, the International Missionary Council (IMC) was declared to be "in association" with it. One of the functions of the World Council was, from the beginning, "to support the churches in their task of evangelism." Since the integration of the International Missionary Council with the World Council in 1961, this function has been expressed comprehensively as follows: "to facilitate the common witness of the churches in each place and in all places," and "to support the churches in their worldwide missionary and evangelistic task." The nearly three hundred member churches in over one hundred countries are committed to this task, and the purpose of this conference is to deepen and further that commitment.

I have been given the daunting task of introducing the work of this conference by indicating the significance of the missionary movement from the meeting of the Edinburgh Conference, June 14–23, 1910, to our meeting here in Melbourne. The seventy years, which we shall rapidly pass in review, have seen radical changes in the world and in the life and witness of the church. These have been noted in the very helpful issue of the *International Review of Mission* of July 1978 on "Edinburgh to Melbourne," and more briefly in the brochure introducing this conference. My only qualification for speaking is that for nearly half of these seventy years I have been involved directly in the work of

*An address to the Melbourne Conference.

9

the International Missionary Council and the Commission on
World Mission and Evangelism, first as missionary secretary of
the British Student Christian Movement in the late 1940s; later as
secretary of the WCC Youth Department with which the IMC was
associated; as a secretary of the Methodist Missionary Society in
London; and as director of CWME. I have had the immense privilege of knowing personally and of having been inspired by several
of the missionary leaders from Edinburgh onward. Perhaps the
most important influence on my life was my own local church on
a small island, Dominica, in the Caribbean. The central event in
our church year was the missionary meeting, and from my earliest
years I was taught to pray for the work of mission and collected
money for the world mission of the church. This sense of belong-
ing to "the Holy Church throughout all the world" and of participating in a small way in the proclamation of the gospel of the
kingdom of God and his justice has been deeply engraved in me,
long before I became acquainted with the vast literature on mission.

Our theme, "Your Kingdom Come," has been at the heart of
the missionary movement throughout Christian history, and not
least in this century. The Student Volunteer Missionary Movement of the late nineteenth century was born in what was called
"The Morning Watch." Prayer and Bible study were the basis of
facing the missionary challenge to proclaim the kingdom to those
who had not heard it. It was in the context of responding to the
demands of the kingdom that people like John R. Mott spoke of
"the evangelization of the world in this generation." As early as
1901 Mott wrote:

> If the Gospel is to be preached to all men it obviously must
> be done while they are living. The evangelization of the
> world in this generation, therefore, means the preaching of
> the Gospel to those who are now living. To us who are re-
> sponsible for preaching the Gospel it means in our lifetime;
> to those to whom it is to be preached it means in their life-
> time. . . . The phrase "in this generation," there-
> fore, strictly speaking, has a different meaning for each
> person.

Mott declared in 1924: "I can truthfully answer that next to the decision to take Christ as the leader and Lord of my life, the watchword has had more influence than all other ideals and objectives combined to widen my horizon and enlarge my conception of the kingdom of God." The Edinburgh Conference did not speak of "the evangelization of the world in this generation," but it was under the deep constraint to get on with the job. At the opening of the conference, the archbishop of Canterbury, Randall Davidson, ended his appeal to his "fellow-workers in the Church Militant, the Society of Christ on earth" with the words:

> The place of missions in the life of the church must be the central place, and none other. That is what matters. Let people get hold of that, and it will tell—it is the merest commonplace to say it—it will tell for us at home as it will tell for those afield. Secure for that thought its true place, in our plans, our policy, our prayers, and then—why then, the issue is His, not ours. But it may well be that if that come true, "there be some standing here tonight who shall not taste of death till they see"—here on earth, in a way we know not now—"the Kingdom of God come with power."[1]

The theme of the kingdom, affirmed in a context of prayer, has been dominant in all the world missionary conferences up to the last one in Bangkok 1972 on "Salvation Today." It is not surprising that the clearest expression of the kingdom was in the prayers that the participants at Bangkok composed as they wrestled with the salvation which Christ offered. Here are excerpts of two prayers:

> Father, so many of the forms of this world are passing away. . . . Help us see that your Son has come into this world to transform it as Lord. . . . Let not this world be changed without me being also changed. Convert me and I shall be converted. Let your judgment come in the Christ who is to come. And let us hasten his coming in the community that seeks his justice. Maranatha. Amen.

O God . . .
You have sent your Son in one place and time,
We praise You!
Be present in every time and place, We pray You!
Your kingdom has come in his salvation, We pray You!
Let it come always among us, We pray you![2]

The first reflection I want to make is that the missionary movement and the world missionary conferences have always been
based on worship, prayer, and Bible study in the presence and
hope of the kingdom. Commentators and critics of the ecumenical movement often forget this profound sense of always being in
the presence of the King and Savior of the world. At Edinburgh
the central act every day was the period of intercession at midday,
apart from other acts of worship. In the message addressed to the
"members of the Christian churches in non-Christian lands," the
last paragraph begins: "A strong co-operation in prayer binds
together in one all the Empire of Christ." Jerusalem 1928, Madras
1938, Whitby 1947, Willingen 1952, Ghana 1957, Mexico 1963,
and Bangkok 1972 were all celebrations of God's kingly rule in
prayer and meditation on his Word. This conference will be in the
same living tradition.

What, then, do we learn from this living tradition of prayerful
reflection and action on the missionary calling of the church to
proclaim in word and act the kingdom of God? I would like to
concentrate on three issues which have impressed themselves on
me in relation to the concerns that are before us in this conference.

The first is the relationship between the kingdom of God and
the kingdoms of this world. The matter can be put in other ways,
like the relationship between salvation history and world history,
or between the text of the gospel of the kingdom and the context
of the world in which the gospel must be preached. (This issue was
only articulated at the Willingen Conference in 1952). What
strikes one forcefully is how difficult our fathers and mothers in
the faith found it, at Edinburgh and Jerusalem particularly, to
relate what was happening in what they called Christian lands to
what was going on in non-Christian lands, as they were fond of
saying.

Let us take the year 1910. The dominant mood of the conference was one of "abounding optimism," as the missionary historian Kenneth Scott Latourette put it. It was the age of Western imperialism. It was the time of "the white man's burden." This phrase was the title of a poem by Rudyard Kipling addressed to the United States to take up their responsibilities as they joined the imperialist club at the end of the nineteenth century. The first verse of that poem says:

> Take up the White Man's burden—
>   Send forth the best you breed—
> Go bind your sons to exile
>   To serve your captives' need;
> To wait in heavy harness,
>   On fluttered folk and wild.—
> Your new-caught sullen peoples
> Half-devil and half-child.

The tone of this verse was that of what was classified as "Social Darwinism." Darwin's books, *On the Origin of Species* (1859) and *The Descent of Man* (1871) had analyzed the human situation as a perpetual struggle for survival, with some races, regarded as superior to others in the evolutionary process, asserting themselves over the weaker races. The English sociologist Herbert Spencer coined the phrase "the survival of the fittest," which he applied to the necessity of the stronger nations, through their industrial, financial, and military power, imposing their will and way over other peoples. At best, these Western empires felt they had a mission, as advanced peoples, to bring civilization to the backward peoples.

The churches and missionary agencies saw it as their duty to bring the best that they had, the gospel, to these peoples as the most effective civilizing influence. The first speaker at the Edinburgh Conference, Lord Balfour of Burleigh, described the great opportunity before the Christian West in these noble terms:

Nations in the East are awakening. They are looking for two things: they are looking for enlightenment and for liberty. Christianity alone of all religions meets these demands in the highest degrees. There cannot be Christianity without liberty, and liberty without at least the restraint of Christian ideals is full of danger. There is a power unique in Christianity of all religions to uplift and to ennoble, and for this reason, that it has its roots and its foundations in self-sacrifice and in love.

Lord Balfour went on to hope that the mission to other countries could well affect relations of nations and churches in the West. He said:

It is a thought not without its grandeur that a unity begun in the mission field may extend its influence and react upon us at home and throughout the older civilizations; that it may bring to us increased hope of international peace among the nations of the world, and of at least fraternal co-operation and perhaps a greater measure of unity in ecclesiastical matters at home.[3]

It is touching to read the record of that conference, which gave such concentrated and dedicated attention to what was happening in Asia, Africa, the Middle East, and the Pacific. But they did not apply their prophetic assessment and judgment to the situation of their own countries and churches, except to lament the lukewarmness of Christians as regards the world mission. And yet the situation in Europe was at that time perilously moving into a cataclysmic conflict. The Western powers were competing with each other for the division of the world for investment, raw materials, and export markets. The doctrine of free trade was described as "the free fox in the free chicken run." But this competition was also expressing itself in the arms race and growing conflict in the West itself. The French socialist Jean Jaurès wrote in 1905:

From a European war a revolution may spring up and the ruling classes would do well to think of this. But it may also result, over a long period, in crises of counter-revolution, of furious reaction, of exasperated nationalism, of stifling dictatorships, of monstrous militarism, a long chain of retrograde violence.[4]

This prophecy has been abundantly fulfilled in these past seventy-five years. It is our present condition in the 1980s—the context in which this conference is being held.

Of course, the participants at Edinburgh were not unaware of these dangers. W. H. T. Gairdner in his interpretation of *Edinburgh 1910* noted recent events that affected the world mission. There was the Boxer Uprising in China in 1900 against the carving up of their country by foreign powers, including Japan. Japan defeated Russia in 1904–5 and trees of victory were planted in several Asian countries. Britain and Russia tried to compose their rivalry by signing an agreement in 1907 in which Tibet was neutralized, Afghanistan was left in the British sphere, Persia was divided in zones of influence with a neutral zone in between. Britain, France, Germany, and Russia were moving inexorably into war.

Another participant in the Edinburgh Conference as a steward was William Temple. He and others had been to a student conference the previous year on "The Social Problem" in class-divided Britain. At the end of the conference, with deep Christian sensitivity, they declared: "*We* are the social problem." That "we" meant the privileged class to which they belonged. The Edinburgh Conference would have gained in depth and relevance if a similar stance could have been taken, because the issues at stake were moral and spiritual. John R. Mott was being perhaps too confident in saying in 1911 that the Edinburgh Conference "has familiarized the Christians of our day with this idea of looking steadily at the world as a whole, of confronting the world as a unit by the Christian Church as a unit." Perhaps this is far truer today than it was then. We can, therefore, be thankful that Mott and his colleagues at least made a beginning.

The point I want to make is that when we are motivated by God's kingly rule, then we are bound, like the Old Testament prophets, to see the world as a whole. The prophets' understanding of God's kingship over the world drove them to declare God's judgment not only on the nations that did not know or accept him, but particularly on Israel as the bearer of his covenant word. For example, Isaiah, who saw the King, the Lord of hosts, in the temple, was renewed to see the world and his own country in a new way—the way of judgment and of hope. That is why he could speak of "that day," the day of the final revelation of God's kingdom, in these beautiful terms:

> In that day there will be a highway from Egypt to Assyria, and the Assyrian will come into Egypt, and the Egyptian into Assyria, and the Egyptians will worship with the Assyrians.
> In that day Israel will be the third with Egypt and Assyria, a blessing in the midst of the earth, whom the Lord of hosts has blessed, saying, Blessed be Egypt my people, and Assyria the work of my hands, and Israel my heritage [Isa. 19:23–25].

I have dwelt on Edinburgh 1910 in order to show the need for relating the text of God's kingdom to the total context of our world and not only as part of it. If time had permitted I could have indicated ways in which the other conferences, including Bangkok, failed to allow the full weight of the kingdom to open their eyes to the missionary task, in its integral relationship of home and abroad. We can be grateful that we, the inheritors of the increasing awareness of Christians over the years, will have an opportunity at this meeting to let the message of the kingdom be our guide for discovering God's mission for the coming years in all its starkness and wholeness.

The second issue I want to bring to your attention is the extraordinary similarity between the concerns debated at Edinburgh and since, up to this meeting. Naturally, these concerns are perceived with greater clarity today, thanks to the boldness and wisdom of our predecessors. I have had an opportunity of consulting not only the reports of the world missionary conferences, but also the minutes of the Continuation Committee after Edinburgh and of the IMC and CWME. It is a heartening and also humbling experience to realize how open these men and women were to what God was leading them to say and to do. I shall refer briefly to several of these concerns.

The Missionary Message

The Edinburgh Conference did not find it necessary to struggle with the missionary message. Christ and their obedience to his call brought the participants together. Lord Balfour, in his opening address, appealed to the trinitarian basis of the faith as Christians sought "to call the human race into one fellowship, to teach the way of eternal life." He said, "The fatherhood of God, the love of the Son, the power of the Holy Ghost, the purity of Christian life, and the splendor of the Christian hope are common ground." There were addresses on "Christianity, the final and universal religion" as redemption and as ethical ideal. Dr. Henry Sloan Coffin, coming out of the Social Gospel tradition, was the one who spoke most fully about the kingdom of God. He said:

> Christianity finds its ethic, as its religion, in Jesus Christ. Its God is the God revealed in Jesus' religious experience—His Father, the eternally Christlike God. Its ethical ideal is the kingdom of that God—the kingdom which Jesus proclaimed and for which He laid down His life. This kingdom is a redeemed social order under the reign of the Christlike God in which every relationship is Christlike, and each individual and social group—the family, the trade-organization, the State—comes not to be ministered unto, but to minister, is perfect as the Father in heaven is perfect, and the whole of human society incarnates the love of God once embodied in Jesus of Nazareth.[5]

The Edinburgh Conference was more concerned with what it described as "a close and continuous study of the position of Christianity in non-Christian lands" and addressed itself mainly to the approach to other faiths. The question could well be asked whether the conference would have been so sure of the message if it had more consciously come to terms with the situation of both church and society in the West. The great insights of the prophets on the character and purpose of the living God came out of the white heat of involvement and struggle with the storms of the world's history around them and beyond.

The Jerusalem Conference had no alternative but to face the challenge of expressing the message of the church in its mission to the world. The carnage of World War I and the bitterness it evoked had destroyed "the abounding optimism" of eighteen years before.

The phrases "Christian lands" and "non-Christian lands"

could no longer be used. Those who dared to proclaim the gospel to people of other faiths would have to do so without reference to any shining examples of countries which nevertheless had had centuries of exposure to the Christian faith. Another factor exposed at Jerusalem was the different ways in which Christians in the West interpreted the Christian message. It was too early to point out that historical and cultural factors influenced this interpretation.

It was interesting that at the end of the long series of papers on Hinduism, Confucianism, Buddhism, Islam, there was one on "Secular Civilization and the Christian Task" by Professor Rufus Jones, who began his paper by saying: "No student of the deeper problems of life can very well fail to see that the greatest rival of Christianity in the world today is not Mohammedanism, or Buddhism, or Hinduism, or Confucianism, but a worldwide secular way of life and interpretation of the nature of things." He added a note: "I am using 'secular' here to mean a way of life and an interpretation of life that include only the natural order of things and that do not find God, or a realm of spiritual reality, essential for life or thought."[6]

Jones significantly ended his paper with the call for a fresh vision of the kingdom of God in terms of daring to live and act according to the prayer of our Lord that God's kingdom come and his will be done on earth as it is in heaven—a position that was hotly debated between Anglo-Saxons and Continentals. Jones appealed to his fellow Westerners:

> Go to Jerusalem, then, not as members of a Christian nation to convert other nations which are not Christian, but as Christians within a nation far too largely non-Christian, who face within their own borders the competition of a rival movement as powerful, as dangerous, as insidious as any of the great historic religions. We meet our fellow Christians in these other countries on terms of equality, as fellow workers engaged in a common task.

It was not surprising that it was the same William Temple, whom I mentioned earlier, who drafted the message which all accepted, though all interpreted it in their own way. In the midst of a world of insecurity and instability, of relativism in human

thought, of suffering and pain, rising nationalism and the yearning for social justice, human brotherhood, and international
peace, the conference declared:

> Our message is Jesus Christ. He is the revelation of what
> God is and of what man through Him may become. In Him
> we come face to face with the ultimate reality of the uni-
> verse; He makes known to us God as our Father, perfect and
> infinite in love and in righteousness; for in Him we find God
> incarnate, the final, yet ever unfolding, revelation of the
> God in whom we live and move and have our being. . . .
>   Christ is our motive and Christ is our end. We must give
> nothing less, and we can give nothing more.[7]

The Minutes of the Committee of the IMC in the years that
followed show that the message was a central concern of the
churches and mission agencies, issuing in an intensive reflection
on the task of evangelism. All this culminated in the great statement of the 1938 Madras Conference on "The Faith by which the
Church Lives," based as it was on the churches all over the world
grappling with the realities around them fearlessly and candidly.
The Madras Conference asserted that "world peace will never be
achieved without world evangelization" and summoned the
churches "to unite in the supreme work of world evangelization
until the kingdoms of this world become the Kingdom of our
Lord."

There have been several expressions of the missionary message
since, and we shall no doubt be adding our own at this conference.
I only want to make a few comments on this effort at articulating
together the message that we proclaim, which might be of some
relevance to us here. First, the biblical revelation has always been
the rallying point of the missionary movement. It was Hendrik
Kraemer who, in his great though controversial book, *The Christian Message in a Non-Christian World* (1938), spoke of biblical
realism. For him the Bible and the Christian faith have an intense
realism that proclaims and asserts realities:

> It does not intend to present a "world view," but it chal-
> lenges man in his *total* being to confront himself with these
> realities and accordingly take decisions. . . . The Bible in its

direct intense realism presents no theology. It presents the
witness of prophets and apostles. . . . To take biblical realism as the fundamental starting point and criterion of all
Christian and theological thinking exposes all problems to
an unexpected and revealing light.[8]

It was in taking seriously the biblical revelation that our understanding of mission has been deepened. The revelation of God is
one of the Father who created the world and humanity in his own
image, who sent his Son to redeem the world and sent his Spirit to
interpret and make real his creative and redemptive work. God is
the true missionary. The mission is God's, not ours. Moreover, as
we have learned since the Willingen Conference of 1952, the basis
of mission is the trinitarian revelation of God in creation, redemption, and fulfillment through Father, Son, and Holy Spirit.
Mission is cosmic in its scope, concerned with bringing the whole
creation and the whole of humanity within the sphere of God's
purpose of good. It is this trinitarian understanding of mission
that enables us to explore fully the meaning of the kingly rule of
God and his justice.

Second, the message must be articulated and communicated in
the context of the culture of people, their whole way of thinking,
believing, and acting. We owe a great debt to the men and women
who clearly perceived from Edinburgh onward the importance of
taking culture and religion seriously. The minutes of the Continuation Committee and of the IMC show what a battle it was to get
the Bible translated, education conducted, and literature produced in the languages of the people. The colonial governments in
many countries were bent on imposing their own language and
culture. The first meeting of the IMC in 1921 enunciated the principle that "Christianity can succeed only as an indigenous movement." Biblical realism demands the encounter with culture and
other faiths in dialogue. Kraemer himself, in the years that followed the Madras Conference, found that he had to speak no
longer of the communication of the faith *to* people of other faiths
and cultures, but rather *with* them. It is in this spirit that we were
able to say at Bangkok, "Culture shapes the human voice that
answers the voice of Christ." It is also in this spirit that dialogue
with people of other faiths and ideologies is conducted. Those

who gathered at Edinburgh in 1910 would rejoice to see the day when there were such rich and varied expressions of the Christian faith around the world and where dialogue with people of living faiths has reached such integrity and depth. Our task is to bring all these experiences and expressions under the judging and renewing purview of the kingdom for the sake of God's mission today.

The Church, Mission, and the Kingdom

At this conference we shall be discussing the church as witnessing to the kingdom, and the kingdom as the raison d'être of the church. At Edinburgh there was a deep conciousness of the need to renew the church to take up its missionary task. The sense of urgency that was sounded there meant, however, mobilizing all the forces of mission in spite of the churches in the West. It was the era of foreign missionary societies and boards supported by a faithful minority in the churches. Exceptions like the Moravians were highly commended. But it was to the churches in the mission lands that the conference issued the most direct appeal: "It is you alone who can ultimately finish this work: the word that under God convinces your own people must be your word; and the life which will win them for Christ must be the life of holiness and moral power, as set forth by you who are men of their race." This was a clear acknowledgment that the church exists for mission and that the base of mission is the local church. It is interesting to observe that it was through the missionary movement that this essential missionary character of the church has become accepted during these years. The World Studies on Churches in Mission and the study on the Missionary Structure of the Congregation in the 1950s and 1960s conducted by CWME have been extremely fruitful for promoting this process.

The debate about the church and the kingdom has in many ways been exaggerated. It is true that there was a tendency in the Byzantine and Roman churches to equate the church with the kingdom, especially as the kingdom was almost equated with the holy empire both East and West. Happily this is no longer a matter of controversy. The missionary movement was reproached for making the church rather than the kingdom the center of mission. A closer study of the documents reveals that what motivated the accent on the church, especially at the Madras Conference in 1938, was not the concern to make the church central, but to call the church to its central evangelistic task through its total life at a time of competing ideologies, of nationalism, and of totalitarian regimes claiming the absolute allegiance of peoples. It was, rather, a valiant attempt at asserting the crown rights of the Redeemer and that the church, which is his body, must transcend all loyalties that may take precedence over the sovereignty of God. This is a challenge that is very much with us in the 1980s and I hope we shall not shirk it in this conference.

What is certainly true is that the eschatological understanding of the kingdom as not only present but to come is a constant call to the church in each place and in all places to renewal and unity. This was clearly stated in the paper prepared for the Second Assembly of the World Council of Churches in 1954 on "Christ—the Hope of the World." It declared:

> Our unity in Christ belongs to the ultimate structure of reality. This is the goal to which all history and all creation move. In pressing forward towards this goal we are one. Let us not forget that when we stand before our Lord at the end we shall stand before our Judge—the Judge of His Church as well as of the world. His judgment will bring about a separation that goes much deeper than all our present divisions and cuts across them all. . . .
>
>   The Church's visible structure passes away with the age, but as the chosen people of God it will enter into the glory of the Kingdom of God that is to come. . . . Here at last the Church will know fully what it is to be one in Christ.[9]

This vital aspect of the relation of the church and the kingdom certainly needs to be carried further in this conference.

Evangelism and Social Concern

At this conference we shall be discussing the plight of the poor, human struggles and power. It has become fashionable in some quarters to be violently critical of CWME and especially of the World Council of Churches for being too concerned with social justice rather than with justification by faith. This kind of criticism has been made since Edinburgh 1910. I am sure, however, that the participants at Edinburgh and at subsequent meetings would endorse the statement at Bangkok:

> The salvation which Christ brought, and in which we participate, offers a comprehensive wholeness in this divided life. We understand salvation as newness of life—the unfolding of true humanity in the fulness of God (Col. 2:9). It is salvation of the soul and the body, of the individual and society, mankind and "the groaning creation" (Rom. 8:19). As evil works both in personal life and in exploitative social structures which humiliate humankind, so God's justice manifests itself both in the justification of the sinner and in social and political justice. As guilt is both individual and corporate so God's liberating power changes both persons and structures. We have to overcome the dichotomies in our thinking between soul and body, person and society, humankind and creation. Therefore we see the struggles for economic justice, political freedom and cultural renewal as elements in the total liberation of the world through the mission of God. This liberation is finally fulfilled when "death is swallowed up in victory" (I Cor. 15:55).[10]

The Edinburgh Conference was confronted with many major social evils that it could not ignore. The opium trade was a matter of deep concern. Bishop Charles Brent, then a missionary in the Philippines, would be chairing an international conference on it at The Hague the following year. He was also the founder of the Faith and Order movement for the unity of the church. At Edinburgh he spoke on the sufficiency of God, which gives courage to dare and courage to bear. Strong reference was made at the meeting to the oppression and wanton destruction to human life being perpetrated in the Congo by the Belgians and their associates. There was a strong discussion on this in the Continuation Committee when apologists for Belgian brutalities tried to say this was beyond the competence of the committee.

At Edinburgh, too, V. S. Azariah of India had raised a very delicate issue which hurt and angered many. He started his address on the problem of cooperation between foreign and national workers as follows: "The problem of race relationships is one of the most serious problems confronting the Church today. The bridging of the gulf between the East and West, and the attainment of a greater unity and common ground in Christ as the great Unifier of mankind, is one of the deepest needs of our time." The Continuation Committee took up the challenge, as it did on such matters as labor relations in new industries in Asia and Africa. J. H. Oldham, that guiding genius of the missionary movement at and after Edinburgh, undertook studies on "Christianity and the Race Problem" (published in 1924), on education, land rights, and industrial labor in Africa. In fact, Oldham was not present at the Jerusalem Conference in 1928 because he considered it top priority for the sake of the gospel and missionary witness that he take part in a commission of inquiry on these matters in East Africa. In the 1920s Oldham, William Paton, and noted economists like R. H. Tawney were drawing attention to the economic and political power structures that maintained racial and social injustices, especially in the poorer nations.

The IMC took a bold step in 1930 by setting up a Department of Social and Industrial Research and Counsel in Geneva. This was strongly contested by some European countries, and Mott and Paton had to find the funds privately to maintain this department under the leadership of the far-seeing, competent, and devoted J. Merle Davis. A monumental volume on the economic basis of the church was prepared for the Madras Conference in 1938.

It was out of the work of this department that such matters as Urban and Rural Mission in CWME and the practical work of organs of the World Council's Unit on Justice and Service sprang.

Moreover, after World War I, when German missions were orphaned, new concerns arose about the relation of missions and governments. Efforts were made to get a clause on religious and missionary freedom in the Convenant of the League of Nations. It was in this context that the missionary leaders in the neutral countries during World War I drew up a statement on the supranationality of missions, which they submitted to diplomatic representatives of the warring powers in 1917. It is interesting to note here that even the most conservative and hostile mission groups appealed to the IMC to help them in matters of religious liberty, and that meant precisely very difficult and protracted political negotiations.

Cooperation and Unity

Perhaps the most difficult issue on the agenda of the missionary movement has been the relations of missions and churches in the evangelistic task. There were two major tasks—to persuade the missionary agencies to work together and to develop relations of partnership with the indigenous churches. At Edinburgh, among the very small band of participants from Asia, two of them challenged the conference in ways that caused deep consternation. Cheng Ching-Yi said: "Speaking plainly, we hope to see in the near future a united Christian Church without any denominational distinctions. . . . The future China will largely depend on what is done at the present time. . . . The Church of Christ is universal, not only irrespective of denominations, but also irrespective of nationalities." V. S. Azariah raised his voice against the racist and paternalistic attitudes of missionaries toward nationals in India and elsewhere. He said to a stunned audience: "You have given your goods to feed the poor. You have given your bodies to be burned. We also ask for love. Give us FRIENDS!"

The Continuation Committee took up the challenge and John R. Mott did much to develop National Christian Councils, particularly in Asia, and to promote better relations between missionaries and nationals. The Jerusalem Conference was the first of its kind in human history when representatives from all over the world could sit together on equal terms. Moreover, one year after the Edinburgh Conference, Mott visited Orthodox Patriarchates and pioneered the participation of the Orthodox in the ecumenical movement. At its meeting in 1912 the Continuation Committee received a report giving statistics on "Missions of the Greek Orthodox Church." A prominent American layman, Silas McBee, had persuaded Monsignor Bonomelli, the Roman Catholic bishop of Cremona, and reputedly a close friend of the pope, to send a message to the conference. This message is a remarkable document, antedating the spirit of Vatican II by over fifty years. He wrote:

> The most desirable and precious of human liberties, religious liberty, may now be said to be a grand conquest of contemporary humanity, and it enables men of various faiths to meet together, not for the purpose of hating and combating each other, for the supposed greater glory of God, but in order to consecrate themselves in Christian love to the pursuit of that religious truth which unites all believers in Christ. United in one faith, the various spiritual forces combine in the adoration of the one true God in spirit and in truth.[11]

We have made valiant efforts over the years to develop relationships in mission that are consonant with our calling as sharing a common life in the body of Christ. At all the world missionary conferences up to Bangkok these issues have been hotly discussed. But we have not got very far in the ecumenical sharing of resources and in our partnership in the gospel. The power of money and of other resources has prevailed. It is our earnest hope that this conference will carry us further along in our quest for true cooperation and unity.

The third major issue I wanted to bring to your attention as we survey these seventy years is the interrelated character of the various parts of the ecumenical movement on mission. The YMCA and YWCA and later the World Student Christian Federation prepared the way for Edinburgh by creating relationships of friendship and cooperation across the barriers of nations, cultures, races, and sexes. Edinburgh 1910 inspired the establishment of the Life and Work movement (1925) and the Faith and Order movement (1927). The work of these movements in turn played a big role in determining the content of the Jerusalem Conference in 1928. Indeed, the 1927 Faith and Order conference statement on the Christian message was incorporated in the Jerusalem statement. J. H. Oldham became the organizer of the World Conference on Church, Community, and State in 1938, which was followed by the Faith and Order Conference. These had a profound influence on the Madras Conference, which itself prepared the way for the active participation of third-world churches and Christians in the formation of the World Council of Churches in 1948 following the Whitby Conference in 1947. The Willingen Conference of 1952 had some effect on the Lund Faith and Order meeting when the principle was enunciated that the churches should act together in all matters except those in which deep differences of conviction compelled them to act separately. And so it has continued until now. The basic conviction behind this was expressed at Amsterdam in 1948 when the World Council of Churches came into being: "The whole Church with the whole Gospel to the whole person in the whole world." One of the purposes of this gathering here in Melbourne is to demonstrate this interrelated character of our calling to mission and to further the cause of mutuality and justice in partnership.

This has been a long pilgrimage, from Edinburgh to Melbourne —and well should it be, because momentous events have taken place both in the world of peoples and nations and in the churches through the missionary movement. What is remarkable about this period is the extraordinary boldness, courage, courtesy, faith, hope, and love displayed by all those who were involved in this great movement. It was William Carey who had said, "Expect great things from God. Attempt great things for God." He was planning a world gathering on mission for 1810 but his dream was not fulfilled until 1910. It was J. H. Oldham who used to say, "We must dare in order to know." In these seventy years many things have been dared in obedience to the gospel of the kingdom of God. We can do no less today.

The times in which we live call for what Bishop Charles Brent said at Edinburgh, "the courage to dare and the courage to bear"—to dare to speak and act for the sake of the kingdom and to bear one another's burdens as those who seek to proclaim and live the way of the kingdom. This is my hope for this conference and for the decisions and actions that will follow. For all this we must begin, continue, and end with the prayer: "Your kingdom come." Over fifty years ago William Paton, that intrepid missionary apostle, ended a book, *The Faith for the World,* with the story of a Telugu girl in India who was learning to pray and who folded her hands and said, "Our Father, our Father, Thy Kingdom, Amen." May this be our prayer throughout this conference.

NOTES

1. *History and Records of the Edinburgh Conference,* p. 150.

2. *Bangkok Assembly,* 1973, pp. 81, 83.

3. *History and Records of the Edinburgh Conference,* p. 145.

4. Jaurés, *Oeuvres,* ed. M. Bannafous. *Pour la Paix* 2 (1931): 247.

5. *History and Records of the Edinburgh Conference,* p. 164.

6. *Jerusalem Report: The Christian Message,* p. 284.

7. Ibid., pp. 480, 486.

8. Kraemer, *The Christian Message in a Non-Christian World* (1938), pp. 64–65.

9. *Report of Advisory Group,* WCC Assembly, 1954, pp. 20, 24.

10. *Bangkok Assembly,* pp. 88–89.

11. W. H. T. Gairdner, *Edinburgh 1910,* p. 210.

Witnessing to the Kingdom

BELLE MILLER McMASTER

In Atlanta, Georgia, I participate in worship on Sunday mornings, surrounded by Tiffany stained-glass windows, moved by the resonant sounds of the pipe organ and the choir singing Bach, cooler than comfortable because of the air conditioning, hearing a sermon and visiting with friends, almost all white and all in "comfortable circumstances." When I pray "Your Kingdom Come," the theme of the Melbourne Conference, I struggle with the meaning of the prayer for myself and the church.[1]

In a rural village in Guatemala a *campesino* (peasant) participates in worship and Bible study in a *comunidad de base*.[2] He interprets the kingdom of God in Isaiah 40:3–5 in this way: "The Lord is already near. He comes, but not even the poor are able to recognize him because they are at the bottom of a pit [*barranco,* deep canyon], the pit of hunger, exploitation, sickness, poverty and injustice. The wealthy exploiters cannot see him either, because their sight is obstructed by their mountains of money, bank accounts, and business."

I in Atlanta and the peasant in Guatamala, with the web of injustices and oppressions that connect and separate us, with the necessities and luxuries I have and the deprivations he endures, and with the heavy irony of a common commitment to Jesus Christ and the coming kingdom of God—there in epitome is the crux of what the Melbourne Conference on World Mission and Evangelism wrestled with as it considered what witnessing to the kingdom means. The central affirmation that gripped the conference was this: *In the perspective of the kingdom, God has a special concern for the poor.* What does that mean for my witness and the witness of other affluent Christians of the world? For the Guatemalan peasant and the poor of the world? If the gospel is good news for the poor, what does it mean for the rich?

While other aspects of the churches' witness to the kingdom were addressed at Melbourne (preaching, the Eucharist, the church as healing community, etc.), I want to offer an interpretation of the significance of this central affirmation of Melbourne about the kingdom and the poor for North American churches: What does it mean for us to pray "Your kingdom come"? What is the church in North America called to do as witness to that kingdom? To put it another way, we shall explore the interface between content (the biblical meaning of the kingdom of God and its special concern for the poor) and context (the implications of that meaning for us).

Your Kingdom Come

In Melbourne people representing a dazzling variety of churches, national identities, racial and ethnic groups, and cultural contexts reflected on the meaning of the kingdom of God. They rejected at least four possible *misunderstandings* of the kingdom theme: (1) since God will bring in the kingdom, we need do nothing; (2) since the kingdom is not of this world, we need only to pray for a heavenly kingdom beyond this world; (3) the kingdom and a just human society are one and the same; (4) the kingdom and the church are one and the same.

Putting these misunderstandings aside, how did the Melbourne Conference understand the kingdom of God? Ernst Käsemann, professor emeritus of New Testament at the University of Tübingen, in presenting the major theological address on the kingdom of God, made four basic points:

1. Through Jesus, crucified and risen, the reign of God begins on earth but is not finally completed.

2. This reign of God means the unmasking of the idols, the humbling of the proud, justice for the oppressed, forgiveness of sins, and redemption from captivity to the powers and authorities.

3. Jesus established signs showing that the kingdom has drawn near and the struggle begun against all who torment and seduce the world and individual human beings and alienate them from their humanity.

4. We in the church are not called to do more, but neither are we called to do less. We are to preach the gospel to every creature

and resist all temptation to noninvolvement in the struggle. Instead of leaving the demonic kingdom in peace, we are to resist it here and there and everywhere. Christians cannot look in neutrality or silence at the appalling inhumanity that is turning the earth into an inferno. This will mean that we face hostility and enmity, but we are liberated and empowered by the experience of the fellowship of Jesus' suffering.

This capsule summary cannot convey the passion of Käsemann's deeply felt convictions about "our earth [as] a kind of hell for the majority of its inhabitants" and the coming kingdom of God. This passion is undoubtedly and appropriately shaped by his experience in Nazi Germany (to which he referred) and by the murder of his daughter, Elisabeth, by Argentine police (to which he did not refer). He said, "The conference and its theme, the kingdom of God, are a provocation for a seventy-four year old man. I cannot resist a provocation so I came. The coming rule of God is *the* political subject of our time. I am a revolutionary but not a socialist. Now at seventy-four I can only understand the church as a resistance movement on earth which has become a hell. The peace of God means war against the tyrants on earth and the ideologies which govern all of us."

Käsemann was pessimistic about the churches of our day, which he believes are enculturated to and blinded by the Western ethos of consumerism. "Christian congregations do not know the situation of the world and do not want to know."

While the conference did not entirely share Käsemann's pessimism about the churches' response, a consistent note was the strong urge to confess the failures of the churches as witnesses to the kingdom of God, especially in light of the second consistent note: the emphasis on the special place God gives to the poor in the kingdom of God.

The emphasis on God's preferential action for the poor caused and will continue to cause debate. Who are the poor? Are the poor those who lack the necessities of life? Do the poor also include those who possess material riches but experience the malaise of technological society, which numbs the spirit? What about those who voluntarily give up possessions to live a life of frugality and self-denial? The temptation to distinguish between material and spiritual poverty was rejected at Melbourne as an inadequate way to understand the situation. Finally, the emphasis was clearly placed on those poor who suffer the lack of the basic necessities of life (the Guatemalan peasant and not myself). The definition offered by the new president of Zimbabwe, the Rev. Canaan Banana, proved to be the most helpful formulation:

> To be poor is to have not, to experience lack and deficiency. . . . The poor are the "little ones" (Mt. 11:25), the insignificant people of no consequence. They are powerless, voiceless and at the mercy of the powerful. . . . The dynamics of the poor are such that the oppressed poor end up accepting the inhumanity and humiliation of their situation; in other words, they accept the status quo as the normal course of life. Thus to be poor becomes both a state of things and an attitude to life, an outlook, even a worldview.

There was also debate over the question, "If the gospel is good news to the poor, is it bad news to the rich?" Melbourne said Yes and No. The good news to the rich is that Jesus Christ issued the call to all to repent and believe in the gospel. The bad news is that those who do not repent, who as the rich allow the face of the poor to be trampled into the dust of the earth, stand before the judgment of God. Melbourne put it this way:

> The good news to the rich confirms what Jesus proclaims as the Gospel for the poor by calling the rich to trust in God and his abundant mercy. It is a call to repentance which means:
> —to renounce the security taken from wealth and material possessions which is idolatry,
> —to give up the exploiting power which is the demonic feature of wealth,
> —to turn away from indifference and enmity over against the poor to solidarity with the oppressed.

In any situation in which there is a conflict between the rich and the poor, the Lord will choose the side of the poor.

Why is there controversy over the poor, the rich, and the kingdom at Melbourne and elsewhere? There are no doubt some good reasons why we cannot agree on who are the poor and worry about the rich, but I want to explore two reasons which I think represent special dangers for North Americans.

In the first place we have a vested interest in the status quo, which makes it easy for us to rationalize what Scripture says about the poor and the rich. Our hermeneutic (interpretation of Scripture) is not disinterested and, indeed, can never be. Interpretation by its very nature reflects the perspective of some person and her or his experience. That reality is neither all positive nor all negative. On the one hand, our experience enables us to enter into and understand the experience of the people of God whose story is told in the Bible. On the other hand, our experience is limited. As those who are not poor and who benefit, sometimes with a cruel innocence, from the poverty of others, our interpretation of Scripture is very likely to be shaped by the rationalization of self-interest.[3]

In the second place, growing out of our vested interests, we have privatized and hence rendered innocuous the gospel of the kingdom of God. As one who belongs to a denomination (the Presbyterian Church in the United States) that was born in the fight over slavery and officially considered the question of slavery outside the realm of the church's concern and even on occasion sought to justify it, I can testify to the pain and destructiveness of the privatization of the gospel in the life of the church even after the church has long since denounced slavery and repudiated a spiritualized gospel. I suspect, indeed I hope, that our comfortable participation in and support of the cruel innocence of the consumer society, which is eating up the world while the cries of the poor and hungry are lost, will be as horrifying to our children's children as my great-grandparents' comfortable participation in and support of slavery is to me. Ernst Käsemann bluntly reminded us of how pervasive is the privatization of the gospel:

> For far too long we have made Christianity into an inward and private affair, . . . at best doing no more than whispering the passionate cry of hope and protest against all that exists: "We have his promise and look forward to new heavens and a new earth, the home of justice" (II Pet. 3:13).[4] The new earth remains a dream; cooperation in

changing the structures is left to outsiders and mostly
fanatics. The proclamation of the resurrection of the dead is
normally, therefore, only a message of personal survival after death for which tombstones are in order but none of the
victory signs which represent a threat to the civil order.

By our watered-down, privatized version of the gospel, the good
news of Jesus is falsified into an opium for the exploited, the
tortured, and the oppressed as well as for the rich and powerful.

The debate over the poor, the rich, and the kingdom of God
signals to us, then, two dangers to the churches, which have the
common result of hindering a faithful witness to the kingdom of
God: (1) interpretation of Scripture and our present situation
from the perspective of the rich and powerful, without the correc-
tive of the voice and experience of the poor, dangerously blinds us
to what God is calling us to do and be; (2) limiting the gospel to
dealing mainly with our private and personal lives without response to the gospel's claim on the public and community aspect
of our lives equally dangerously blinds us to what God is calling us
to do and to be.

The Poor and the Churches' Witness

Maria Gwata of Zimbabwe, U Kyaw Than of Burma, Orlando
Costas of Costa Rica, John Brown of Australia, Lois Miller of the
United States, Halina Bortnowska of Poland—together more
than five hundred of us—men and women, black, brown, and
white, Asian, African, Latin American, North American, European, Protestant, Roman Catholic, and Orthodox, representing
churches of many confessions, from capitalist, socialist, and
Third World countries, searched, sometimes in pain and struggle,
for the implications of God's preference for the poor for the witness of the church. It was clear to us that the church is called to
solidarity with the poor. But what does it mean for affluent
churches to identify with the poor?

Style of Mission

Our style of mission must continue to move away from
domination by the richer churches of the northern hemisphere.

Melbourne insisted that the poor are already in mission to change their own situation. "What is required of the churches is a missionary movement that supports what the poor have already begun. . . . The churches will need to surrender their attitudes of benevolence and charity by which they have condescended to the poor; in many cases this will mean a radical change in the institutional life of the missionary movement."

While Melbourne reemphasized the necessity of mutuality in mission between the financially richer churches in the northern hemisphere and the financially poorer churches in the southern hemisphere, it suggested that mission in the decades ahead may take place increasingly within each hemisphere rather than across hemispheres. Stronger initiatives will come from the churches of the poor and oppressed in Asia, Africa, and Latin America with increasing traffic among these churches. This new reality "could well result in the loosening of the bond of domination and dependence that so scandalously characterizes the relationship between many churches of the Northern and Southern Hemispheres respectively." Many of us have learned the language of "partnership" and "mutuality in mission," but we have not been able to live out the reality.

Solidarity with the Poor and the Ideological Captivity of the Church

Melbourne called the churches to "dare to be present at the bleeding points of humanity . . . even taking the risk of being counted among the wicked." There is always the temptation on the part of the churches, especially affluent churches, to avoid taking sides because of the ambiguities of the struggle. The ambiguities are a reality that we must not overlook. When the church supports proximate solutions, it must never make the mistake of believing they are ultimate solutions. Our danger, however, is not that we shall identify some other social order with the kingdom of God but that we shall fail to recognize the ideological captivity of the church to the present social and economic order.

Melbourne was clear about the danger of ideological conformity by any church. It issued warnings to churches in capitalist, socialist, and Third World countries. In speaking to the use of

Marxist analysis, the conference illustrated the dangers, using the experience of the church under capitalism:

> If a church or members of a church should choose to use Marxist or any other ideological instruments to analyze the social, economic and political situation in which they find themselves, it will be necessary to guard against the risk of being subtly instrumentalized by such ideologies so as not to fall into the same trap as many churches have done in relation to the ideology implied by capitalism and thus lose their fidelity to the Gospel and credibility.

The ideological captivity of the American churches is, in my judgment, the most serious issue presently facing the church. Melbourne described the consumer culture to which we are captive: "A vast fertility cult expects a wild, egotistical increase, demanding human sacrifice as the price of building our industrial cities in rich and poor countries alike for the economic benefit of a minority of individuals."

The basis of our ideological captivity has been perceptively analyzed by Walter Brueggemann: "The contemporary American church is so largely enculturated to the American ethos of consumerism that it has little power to believe or act." The present order, he says, like that of Pharaoh and Solomon, is supported by an interlocking *economics of affluence, politics of oppression,* and *religion of a captive God.* Against this "royal consciousness," Moses, the prophets, and Jesus offer an alternative consciousness: the *economics of equality,* the *politics of justice,* and the *religion of God's freedom.* What Brueggemann calls the "royal consciousness" serves as a counterwitness to the kingdom of God, whereas the "alternative consciousness" is an authentic witness to the kingdom of God. Both the prophets and Jesus

> bring to expression and embodiment all the hurt, human pain, and grief that the dominant royal culture has tried to repress, deny and cover over. . . . The one thing the dominant culture cannot tolerate or coopt is compassion, the ability to stand in solidarity with the victims of the present order. It can manage charity and good intentions, but it has no way to resist solidarity with pain or grief.[5]

The dismaying reality is that the majority of church people in North America see no conflict between an affluent consumer culture and the kingdom of God and are largely numbed to the hurt, human pain, and grief of the poor. So long as that is true, we shall not be able, as churches, to stand in solidarity with the poor or be faithful witnesses to the kingdom.

Spirituality and the Powers of Exploitation and Impoverishment

A new emphasis at Melbourne was a deepened recognition of the fundamentally spiritual nature of the conflict with the powers of exploitation and impoverishment.

Raymond Fung, who works in urban-industrial mission in Hong Kong, pointed to the spiritual nature of what happens to the victims of exploitation and impoverishment:

A person persistently deprived of basic material needs and political rights is a person deprived of much of his or her soul—self-respect, dignity and will. A fisherman deprived of his waters, a peasant of his land becomes a person deprived physically and spiritually. . . . I cannot forget the faces of the poor who sat on the ground helpless, seeing their homes bulldozed away to make way for a summer resort. There was almost a visible resentment and hatred on their faces, which turned inward and gnawed at their own soul. The destroyer of the body may not be able to kill the soul, but it can, and too often does, rape and maim the soul.

Fung, affirming the horror and reality of sin in human lives and human institutions, argued that the gospel not only calls on people to repent of their sins but also to resist the forces that sin against them. The church is called to communicate the gospel for the *sinned-against* as well as the *sinner*. Just as the physical impoverishment of the poor is a spiritual matter, so also is the fight against the forces of exploitation.

There were no simple answers offered for the battle against the forces of exploitation. A sober sense of reality coupled with the recognition of the deeply spiritual nature of the issues made the prayer "Your kingdom come" the heartfelt response of those gathered at Melbourne. The prayer, sung and recited again and again, became a sustained cry of yearning for the coming of the kingdom, gratitude for whatever evidences are already present in society, and faith that God will bring the kingdom in all its fullness.

There was also no retreat from specific programmatic proposals to work for a new international economic order, to challenge the transnationals, to take sides in the human rights struggles under repressive regimes, to challenge the dangerously escalating militarism, and to change our lifestyles in the world.

But there was no forgetting that we wrestle not with flesh and blood but with principalities and powers. Emilio Castro, director of the WCC Commission on World Mission and Evangelism, summed it up, "We are in a spiritual struggle. . . . The struggles to overcome economic, social, and political manifestations should be considered on their own merit. But at the root there is a spiritual reality: principalities, powers of evil that need to be combatted with spiritual powers and spiritual realities: the power of love, the power of hope, the power of the Gospel."[6]

We are in a spiritual struggle, which in many places requires the church to take up the cross and suffer. Testimony was given at Melbourne to the suffering, imprisonment, and even martyrdom of Christians in many parts of the world. Indeed, said Melbourne, "The marks of the crucified Christ will determine the social action of the church and its members." We, in the churches in North America, shaped by what Bishop John V. Taylor called "the doctrine of achievement"[7] and characteristically concerned for pragmatic solutions, will find it very hard even to recognize the marks of the cross, much less bear them. The expectation of "success" for the pastor or lay person is so insidiously built into even the church that we tend to regard as a "failure" anyone who does not fit into the established pattern, who offends too many people, who is too angry. If one must "succeed" to be valued in the church, how can we expect as a church to bear the marks of the cross in society?

Power and Church Structures

In its response to the oppression of the poor, Melbourne noted that the church is forced to recognize the misuse of power within and by its own institutions and the reluctance of the church to risk its institutional life for the poor.

Two criteria were proposed for judging whether or not the exercise of power is a witness to the kingdom: (1) Is the power primarily used in behalf of the needs of the poor and the powerless? (2) Is power shared within the church both in decision-making and in the exercise of all the gifts of ministry?

The most difficult issue proved to be the sharing of power within the church where structures of domination more often reflect society than the servant model of Jesus. Women at the conference experienced firsthand the failure to share power in a male-dominated church. They said, "Women have been told by those in power how to serve the Lord and men. The 'church fathers' have told the 'church mothers' what to do and why." When serious questions were raised about the validity of hierarchical patterns in the structure of the church, differences of opinion were so sharp that the word "hierarchical" was struck and "pyramidical" substituted. However, the conference urged further exploration of the unresolved ecumenical debate over the validity of hierarchy largely at the insistence of women, whose experience on the periphery of power has given them the perspective of the marginalized. The point most emphasized by women was that the misuse of power in the structures and organization of a male-dominated, hierarchical church is an impediment to the mission and witness of the church. An unrecognized, invisible ministry of service is and has been the experience of women for centuries, but women envisioned the coming of a shared community of women and men that would release new energy for witness.

There was an attempt by men from the Third World to argue that the issue of the liberation of women is a North American/ European problem that has no bearing for other cultures. Third World women resolutely resisted this analysis and testified to their own oppression. If the church cannot learn within its own institution to share power with the women in its midst, there is little likelihood that the church will be able to share power with the poor. The reality is that around the world the poorest of the poor are women. They desperately need the necessities of life, the affirmation of their gifts, and the church as the voice of their voicelessness.

We return to the question that will be central for the churches of North America in the next decades, the question that gripped the hearts and minds of those gathered at Melbourne: What does it mean for an affluent church to witness to the kingdom in solidarity with the poor?

- It means a new direction for partnership in mission, with initiative coming from the churches of the poor.
- It means taking sides in the struggle of the poor even at the risk of being wrong.
- It means repenting of the ideological captivity of the church to the culture.
- It means acknowledging the deeply spiritual nature of the battle against the powers of exploitation and impoverishment.
- It means suffering as a church on behalf of a suffering world.
- It means risking the institutional power of the church for the poor and the powerless.
- It means sharing the responsibility of power within the church so that no group is excluded and all may exercise their gifts of ministry as a witness to the new community of the kingdom.
- It means praying together, Your kingdom come!

NOTES

1. Throughout this chapter the word "church," unless otherwise noted, refers to the dominant white church in North America. An analysis from the black church perspective, for example, would be quite different.

2. Base Christian communities are "organized inside the Roman Catholic Church among the poor, both in large cities and in the countryside. Led by lay catechists and priests who have determined to live among the poor, these groups are able to study the Bible together, share the Eucharist, develop common actions and strengthen the people of their communities in the struggle against injustice." All quotations, unless otherwise identified, are drawn from the documents and addresses of the WCC Conference on World Mission and Evangelism, Melbourne, Australia, May 12–24, 1980. Texts are available from the World Council of Churches, 150 route de Ferney, 1211 Geneva 20, Switzerland.

3. See Robert McAfee Brown, *Theology in a New Key* (Philadelphia: Westminster Press, 1978), pp. 77–88, for a discussion of ways to recognize and offset our biases in Scripture interpretation.

4. Note that Käsemann translates the word "righteousness" in 2 Pet. 3:13 as "justice," a more accurate English rendering. In the Old Testament justice and righteousness are nearly synonymous and often appear together in parallel form. That meaning of righteousness as justice carries over into the New Testament. Righteousness in English, however, has come to mean general moral uprightness or virtuousness, especially in the sense of individual morality, and has lost the biblical meaning of justice. See Belle Miller McMaster, "Prisons and Preachers," *Journal for Preachers* 3, no. 2 (1980): 14–16.

5. See Walter Brueggemann, *The Prophetic Imagination* (Philadelphia: Fortress Press, 1978), pp. 11, 87–88. Brueggemann moves helpfully from the paradigm of royal consciousness and alternative consciousness to consider concretely what the implications are for prophetic ministry today.

6. If there ever was any truth to the charge that the World Council of Churches is primarily an activist organization concerned only with politics and not also with spirituality, that charge is no longer true based on the evidence of the Melbourne Conference, which recognized that politics and spirituality cannot be separated for the believer.

7. Taylor said, "The doctrine of achievement has produced our modern, efficiency oriented society in which people are constrained to make progress and be successful in order to justify themselves." The doctrine of achievement, said Taylor, reflects the world's values and is supported by a distorted Christianity, but is fundamentally in opposition to the lifestyle of the kingdom of God.

The Fullness of Mission

WALDRON SCOTT

God doesn't deal in half measures. In his presence, the psalmist declares, is fullness of joy. When Jesus came to earth all the fullness of God was pleased to dwell in him. Saint John assures us that from Jesus' fullness we all have received grace piled upon grace. And Jesus himself testified, "I came that they might have life, and have it *abundantly*" (cf. Isa. 6:3; Ps. 16:11; Col. 1:19; Jn. 1:16; 10:10).

Why is it, then, that down through history Christians have tended to dilute this rich, full mission of God—to domesticate it, dichotomize it, enfeeble it, reduce it to "manageable" proportions, color it gray, make of it no more than one of its parts?

The earliest believers thought to limit God's mission to Jews only. Roman regents attempted to harness it to imperial interests. Hermits interiorized it. Mystics etherealized it. Crusaders reduced it to barbarity. Reformers circumscribed it. "The parish is my world," they insisted. In the nineteenth century missionaries linked it uncritically to colonial concerns. In the twentieth century a few have even placed it at the service of the CIA.

Thank God others, even in our own time, have seen more clearly the multidimensional nature of mission. The apostle Paul understood, in a way his contemporaries did not, that the gospel was for all the nations, not just Israel. Saint Francis of Assisi saw that there was *work* to be done among the poor. Not only humanity but nature is redeemable in God's great plan of salvation. Ignatius Loyola reached out to all nations, while John Wesley turned the Reformers' dictum on its head, boldly asserting, "The world is my parish!" More recent history is replete with missionaries who courageously opposed mercantilist crimes and political perversions.

Throughout the twentieth century, nevertheless, we have struggled to apprehend the fullness of mission—or allow it to apprehend us. Our grapplings have not been altogether futile. We have discovered deeper meanings of salvation. We have come to appreciate the complexities of mission. We have pioneered new frontiers of joint action. Yet by and large we have proved ourselves unequal to the challenge. Great areas of geography and culture are still unreached by the gospel. We have allowed the pendulum to oscillate from evangelism to social action and back again. We have polarized the body of Christ to an unnecessary and even self-defeating degree.

The 1980 Conference on World Mission and Evangelism in Melbourne contributed a great deal to our understanding of the fullness of mission. The Melbourne meeting focused on the kingdom of God—probably the most fruitful symbol of mission in Scripture. Melbourne directed our attention to the poor and their struggles for justice. It emphasized the biblical demand for authenticity in the churches' witness. It introduced some of us to unexpected dimensions of mission in the Eastern Orthodox tradition. Above all, it challenged the church to a new style of mission in the power encounters of our time.

Yet Melbourne did not escape the bias to reduce mission to something less than the sum of its parts. While Melbourne had much to say about how we are to witness to the kingdom in areas where the church *exists,* it was virtually silent on how we are to carry out mission where the church *is not yet*. And in truth there are hundreds of thousands of towns and villages, in Asia especially, where the church is not present in any form. There are unreached peoples, hidden peoples, numbering two-thirds of the world's population, for whom cross-cultural missions (evangelistic, church-planting, disciple-making missions) are still prerequisite. Melbourne wrongly down-played missions in these traditional terms, thereby depleting the fullness of mission.

In the remainder of this chapter I would like to discuss cross-cultural missionary activity in the light of what was given to us at Melbourne.

Good News to the Poor

Missionary vocation during the past two centuries has expressed itself in terms of masses of individuals, dark continents, inscrutable religions, or, more recently, hidden peoples. "There are 2.7 billion persons who have yet to hear the name of Jesus," we are told. Or, "God has called me to Africa." Again, "My mission is to reach Muslims." Or, "Our strategy must focus on the 11,300 unreached people groups." Each of these approaches is legitimate in its own way. Yet Melbourne reminded us that the Lord Jesus announced at the beginning of his own mission that God had anointed him especially to preach good news to *the poor* (cf. Lk. 4:18). The poor are still the largest unreached people[1] in the world. Emilio Castro, director of the WCC Commission on World Mission and Evangelism, affirms that "the fact that so many poor people in the world do not have any access to this knowledge of God's grace in Jesus Christ is a challenge to our Christian conscience."[2]

Some missionary theorists today argue against the poor constituting a people group (with the attendent obligation to develop a specific strategy for reaching them). They suggest that there really isn't enough homogeneity within "the culture of poverty" to include the poor in general as a people group. But why then is "the poor" such a prominent category in Scripture? Is it not precisely because of the homogeneity of the needy? Important distinctions can be made between the relatively poor and the absolutely poor, and between the rural poor and the urban poor. Yet the poor everywhere are alike in that they lack money, they are underemployed (or employed not at all), they have inadequate nutrition, housing, health and educational opportunities, and they experience chronic feelings of powerlessness, insignificance, frustration, and despair.

It will not do to contrast "the poor" (Lk. 6:20) with "the poor in spirit" (Mt. 5:3) too sharply. Still less may we apply the gospel to the one rather than the other. The Rev. Canaan Banana, president of Zimbabwe, rightly notes that to be poor is both a state of being and an attitude to life. Lack of food, shelter, and clothing produces spiritual anguish and physical misery. Lack of love can make even the most affluent material circumstances unbearable. God intends for all humanity to have both the material and cultural necessities of life *and* that assurance of personal, spiritual well-being that comes from being reconciled to God and to our fellow human beings.

Poverty is a pervasive feature of our world today—perhaps its most pervasive feature.[3] A Guatemalan *campesino* (peasant) in a rural Bible study group commented on Isaiah 40:3-5 this way: "The Lord is already near. He comes, but not even the poor are able to recognize him because they are at the bottom of a pit (barrancos = deep canyons), the pit of hunger, exploitation, sickness, poverty and injustice" (Section I, 9).

Responding to the commission to preach the gospel to the poor opens up exciting new dimensions of mission. It casts new light on our missionary *statistics*. It forces us to rethink our missionary *message*. It challenges our missionary *style*.

The Statistics of Missions

Statistically, we know that one-seventh of the world's population is Muslim; one-sixth is Indian; one-fifth is Chinese. Together these three groups constitute most of the "unreached peoples" of the world, as that phrase is being used currently. An even more important statistic, however, is this: four-fifths of the world's population is poor, impoverished—millions of them desperately impoverished—materially, culturally, spiritually. As we seek to reach the unreached we dare not ignore this reality. In the global context the poor are not small minorities clustered here and there. The poor are the *vast majority*.[4]

This is difficult for many Americans to grasp, so cocooned are we from the desperate plight of our fellow human beings: an island of affluence in an ocean of poverty. But grasp it we must. For as James, the Lord's brother, tells us pointedly, God has chosen the marginalized of the world to be rich in faith and heirs of the kingdom that he has promised to those who love him (cf. Jas. 2:5). In other words, God knows the poor are uniquely responsive to the gospel. They are the natural citizens of the kingdom. Thus Section I at Melbourne declared, "The churches cannot neglect this evangelistic task. Most of the world's people are poor and they are waiting for a witness to the gospel that will really be 'good news.' "

Moreover, in many parts of the world today the poor and powerless are in the vanguard of those proclaiming the kingdom. They are not mere objects of mission so much as subjects—active participants. This is so in Hong Kong factories, in African independent churches, in Brazilian base communities, and in countless other situations. When an upheaval occurs in a society the poor remain to witness while the middle classes often flee. (Fifty-nine out of sixty-two Methodist pastors fled Cuba at the time of the revolution.) For the witness of the gospel to remain strong in a country it must be rooted among the weak.

In India a worker from one of the indigenous missionary societies has been living among palm-tree tappers. He finds that they are being charged huge interest rates on small loans from moneylenders. They know nothing about assistance programs the government has set up. The Indian missionary therefore sets about making the tappers aware of their exploitation and the availability of help. The tappers become conscious of new, alternative patterns of human relationships. When the question arises of how these new patterns can be achieved, the story of Christ and the reconciliation he provides between God and human and between person and person moves to the top of the agenda.

Saint Paul informs us that God desires all human beings to be saved and to come to knowledge of the truth (cf. 1 Tim. 2:4). The apostle Peter confirms this, noting that God does not wish that any should perish, but that all should reach repentance (cf. 2 Pet. 3:9). Most of the "all" and "any" referred to in these passages are poor people. Yet many of our modern missionaries focus their attention on the rich. Often they do not see themselves as serving the rich. They speak instead of reaching university students or middle-class professionals in Third World countries,[5] overlooking the fact that in these countries university students are the future rich, and professionals form a tiny, highly privileged sector of society. The middle class, where it exists in developing countries, almost always is allied with the rich and powerful.

Missionaries focusing on students, professionals, and well-to-do businessmen defend their strategy, of course. They suggest that by reaching the highly educated, the leaders of society, the pace-setters, they will more quickly reach the masses of poor people. This highly dubious proposition has little warrant in history and less in Scripture. It seems to be simply another application of the long-since discredited "trickle down" theory in economics. I suspect that in many instances missionaries working among the tiny middle classes in non-Western societies do so because they themselves come from middle-class backgrounds or perceive themselves to be upwardly mobile. They just feel more comfortable among middle-class people than among the poor.

On the other hand, missionaries who do work among the poor must not be content to dole out charity. Nor can they engage in that kind of "development" that allows for only a limited number of the poor to join the middle-class elite without working to overcome societal injustice for the many.

The Missionary's Message

If, as Melbourne suggested, an essential part of missionary activity is proclaiming the kingdom of God, many of us will have to rethink our message. We are likely to discover that the gospel we preach is one-dimensional. It does injustice to the fullness of mission expressed by the kingdom. In contemporary jargon, it needs to be "contextualized"—made relevant to a specific situation and a specific moment in history.

What is the good news we have to share with the poor and oppressed in their context? As an initial announcement it can be expressed in the familiar words of Campus Crusade's first spiritual law: "God loves you and has a wonderful plan for your life!" Such an announcement is certainly news to the poor. All the experiences they have accumulated in a lifetime of oppression seem to point in the opposite direction. Most are convinced from what they see around them that God loves the *rich* and has a marvelous plan for *their* lives!

Yet the Bible clearly teaches otherwise. We have already noted James' teaching that God has chosen poor people to be rich in faith and heirs of the kingdom. This is good news. The apostle Paul reminds the Corinthian believers, most of whom were from the poorer classes (cf. 1 Cor. 1:26–29), of the grace of our Lord Jesus Christ: "though he was rich, yet for your sake he became poor, so that by his poverty you might become rich" (2 Cor. 8:9). God is not only *for* the poor but *with* them in Jesus Christ.

God first revealed his preference for the poor in the history of his dealings with Israel. When they were slaves he heard their cry and came to deliver them (cf. Exod. 3:7-8). He led them out of oppression into the promised land where dignity, self-determination, and equity would characterize their national and interpersonal relationships. Through his prophets God never allowed Israel to forget that his kingdom was for the poor. The first sentence of our missionary message, then, is that the Ruler of the universe, the Creator of all things, is the Friend and Redeemer of the weak and powerless. In Raymond Fung's memorable phrase, God sides with "the sinned-against."

The second sentence is that the Friend is also the Judge. This is no small thing. God not only loves the poor; he hates evildoers (cf. Ps. 34:16). In Scripture evildoers (Hebrew: *reshaim*) are those who oppress the poor and the needy (cf. Ps. 73:1-14). In the great struggles of our day God actively sides with the poor and oppressed. As Mary the mother of our Lord saw clearly, in his kingdom the mighty fall and the lowly are lifted up (cf. Lk. 1:52).

We can be more specific. God is on the side of those who struggle for liberation and self-determination in the political context. God supports those who struggle for basic human rights. Any socioeconomic system that denies basic needs is unjust and inevitably opposed by God. God stands against the economic principalities and powers of our age, those great multinational corporations, the pride of American enterprise, wherever they exploit the poor. God opposes our democratic parliaments and congresses whenever they perpetrate legal injustice by "stacking the deck" in favor of the haves against the have-nots. According to the psalmist, this is framing mischief by decree (cf. Ps. 94:20). The poor eke out their existence in a world created by evil people and condoned by good people. Thus the mission of the Lord Jesus himself is said to be a mission of rectification, of establishing justice (cf. Isa. 42:1-4; Mt. 12:18-21).[6]

In all honesty, though, there is a third sentence. The oppressed are themselves oppressors. The sinned-against are also sinners. A laborer toils all week long at a monotonous, demeaning task, exploited by the rich and powerful. Devoid of meaning and purpose in life, despairing of hope for the future, he squanders his meager wages on alcohol, then returns home to beat his wife. She in turn, cooped up in a crowded tenement flat, with no mobility or cultural outlet, vents her frustration on her children—who kick the cat!

All of us, therefore, rich and poor alike, need forgiveness. We all sin against our fellow human beings and such sin is sin against God. We are thereby alienated not only from our fellow human beings but from God. We need to be reconciled to God. This reconciliation was effected at Calvary. There God's Son, the only sinless person who ever lived, became the supremely sinned against one. On the cross he bore the sins of all humankind—not just the petty misdemeanors religious people so often preoccupy themselves with, but the horrendous, outrageous sins of society's institutions as well.

Moreover, all of us, rich and poor alike, face the ultimate enemy, death. In death hopes are haunted, dreams demolished, loved ones torn apart. By his resurrection Jesus conquered death and invested our individual efforts and relationships with eternal significance. Through Jesus' death and resurrection God's kingdom of peace, freedom, joy, justice, and eternal life is offered to all. By a personal, individual faith-commitment to Jesus as Lord and Savior we enter the kingdom. All of the promises of the kingdom—both now and beyond death—are ours in Christ (cf. 2 Cor. 1:20).

Section III at Melbourne declared that "the story of God in Christ is the heart of all evangelism, and this story has to be told. . . . The telling of the story is an inescapable mandate for the whole church; word accompanies deed as the kingdom throws its light ahead of its arrival and men and women seek to live in that light."

At the same time, to enter the kingdom is to enlist in the service of the King. The risen King, as we have seen, is engaged in a continuing struggle with the principalities and powers of darkness. His arena, in the words of Albert Camus, is the blood-stained face of history. To this end he has called into existence a community, the community of the King, to work with him to establish justice on the earth. Within this new community the power of the Holy Spirit is released. Spiritual gifts are discovered, developed, and deployed in the ministry of reconciliation. Those who struggle alongside the poor are empowered by the Spirit to persevere, even in the face of persecution, imprisonment, and death. They overcome by the blood of the Lamb and by the word of their testimony (cf. Rev. 12:11).

The good news we proclaim to the poor and dispossessed, in

summary, consists of the announcement that God is both Friend and Judge, that in righteous love he assists the lowly and opposes the mighty, and that in the Calvary event he provides a definitive reconciliation—vertical and horizontal—for all who will respond. He therefore calls individuals to repentance and faith, and offers forgiveness, spiritual power, and eternal life. He further calls men and women to a community committed to the pursuit of wholeness here and now. This is the life of discipleship. This is what Jesus had in mind when he commissioned us to "make disciples of all nations" (Mt. 28:19).

The Style of Missions

Such a message requires a special style. It calls for radical changes in the direction of the contemporary missionary movement, in our missionary institutions, in the kind of missionary required, and in our approach to preparation and training.

Direction

American Christians still have not abandoned the image of missionary activity as one-way traffic. From us to them. From West to East. From North to South.[7] From Christendom to the heathen. From developed countries to underdeveloped countries. This image falsifies the reality of our time. It fails to recognize that the churches of Asia, Africa, and Latin America have matured. They are increasingly disenchanted with the quality of "Christian" life in Europe and North America. In their maturity Third World Christians naturally identify more directly with the socioeconomic aspirations of their fellow citizens. They are becoming aware of the cause-effect relationship between the policies of the Christian West (or North) and their own desperate situations. Moreover, in their maturity they are discovering the Great Commission for themselves and developing their own missionary agencies. Theodore Williams, himself an Indian missionary executive, calls these "the emerging missions."[8]

So it is no longer us *to* them, but us *with* them—and, significantly, *between* them and them! This new form of missionary movement is still embryonic. But who can doubt that it is the wave of the future? Section IV at Melbourne reported: "While not in any way denying the continuing significance and necessity of a mutuality between the churches in the northern and southern hemispheres, we believe that we can discern a development whereby mission in the eighties may increasingly take place within these zones. . . . There will be increasing traffic between the churches of Asia, Africa and Latin America. . . . "

At Melbourne the Japanese theologian Kosuke Koyama drew attention to still another vector in the missionary movement. Jesus was crucified "outside the gate" (Heb. 13:12)—that is, at the periphery of society. He who is the center of the whole universe, he who is at the center of all human life, is constantly in movement from the center toward the periphery—toward those who are marginalized, victims of demonic powers, whether they be political, economic, cultural, or even religious.

If we take this model seriously missionaries must be with Jesus at the periphery. Thus the author of the letter to the Hebrews exhorts, "Let us go forth to him outside the camp, bearing abuse for him. For here we have no lasting city, but we seek the city which is to come" (Heb. 13:13–14). Since the countries of the South, their poverty-trapped masses, and their churches are themselves at the periphery of our contemporary world order, Koyama's model and Melbourne's response are consistent with what we have discussed to this point.

Institutions

Where Western missionary agencies are concerned, the changes of which we are speaking point in the direction of more effectual partnerships with Third World churches. Some mission agencies, such as the century-old Sudan Interior Mission (SIM), have demonstrated great sensitivity in developing such relations. In response to critical felt needs SIM has strengthened its human development program while maintaining its historical emphasis on evangelism and church planting. SIM has developed a full range of on-site training programs for pastors of the Evangelical Churches of West Africa (ECWA). And without infringing on the prerogatives of ECWA it has quietly assisted ECWA to create its own missionary society, the Evangelical Missionary Society

(EMS). It may surprise the reader to learn that the EMS now supports over two hundred missionary couples, working entirely under African supervision, evangelizing across numerous cultural frontiers in West Africa.

Such partnership is essential for the future. We speak rightly and even urgently of nearly 3 billion persons who have yet to hear the gospel in any significant way. And we instinctively call for a dramatic expansion of Western missionary forces. But the great majority of those who have never heard of Jesus today are Muslims, Indians, and Chinese—precisely the peoples least accessible to Western missionaries. There is a strange contradiction here, one that Western missions for the most part have not faced up to.

If most of the unreached live in China, India, and Muslim lands (these areas contain 60 percent of the world's population)—and if these lands are closed to large-scale Western missionary enterprise—why are we talking about the multiplication of Western missionaries? Such missionaries would necessarily have to be deployed where the church has already been established. Asian, African, and Latin American churches can perhaps withstand the impact of modest increases in Western missionaries. Anything more than modest increases will "swamp the boat" and result in understandable calls for a moratorium on missionaries.

On the other hand, are we to abandon the missionary enterprise? No, of course not—not when so many millions still wait for the good news of the kingdom. While Western missionaries are still needed in some places, *non*-Western missionaries may be even more essential. If so, then the phenomenon of "emerging missions" referred to above takes on fresh import while the demand for genuine partnership between Western and non-Western missionary agencies acquires new force.

Is such partnership possible? An increasing number of Western missionary agencies consciously or unconsciously model themselves on the modern multinational corporation. In such cases institutional control, finances, and decision-making—in other words, power—are kept in the hands of the Western agency. In a disturbing number of instances some of the brightest leaders of the national churches are lured away by the higher salaries and the greater mobility offered by Western agencies. In the name of the

Great Commission the churches—fruit of decades of missionary labor—are weakened, sometimes disastrously. All this merely perpetuates the worldly values of our era and works against the kingdom while purporting to extend it.

On the one hand, our missionary enterprise is supported by the sacrificial prayers, labor, and money of thousands of ordinary Christians. On the other hand, as Melbourne pointed out, it is frequently financed by the fruits of exploitation. It is sometimes conducted in league with oppressive governments and multinational corporations. And it is too often carried out with little regard to the structural environment of those who are the object of missionary endeavor.

Too often Western agencies—even some emerging missions that mistakenly pattern themselves after Western agencies— concentrate on empire building. Each maintains its own office, recruits its own staff, buys its own equipment, and carves out its own territory (functional or geographical). Meanwhile important opportunities for developing the capacity for effective cooperation and joint action at local and regional levels are lost. Lip service is paid to cooperation while each agency continues to do its own thing. Hasn't the time come for Christ's body to begin functioning like a body, for Christ's team to begin working as a team?

Missionaries

In this transitional period of missions a new breed of missionary is called for. Recently I received a newsletter from a young missionary-to-be. In the letter he laid out his financial needs. Nearly $20,000 cash is required to transfer him, his wife, and small child to their intended location and get them settled in. Once that is accomplished he estimates $30,000 a year will be required to provide for his family and for a modest ministry. Such expenditure—not at all uncommon for American missionaries today— raises serious questions. Can rich people really communicate with poor people? Can a $30,000-a-year lifestyle truly mirror the kingdom of God in a developing country? Is it possible to avoid overtones of superiority and condescension, of power and domination, in the relationship between a $30,000-a-year Western missionary and his partner, a $3,000-a-year national missionary?

Can we learn to live simply? Can we learn to do missionary work apart from an almost obsessive reliance on technology? Not that modern technology is to be despised. Yet we must face up to the impact that sophisticated equipment, owned and controlled by one partner in a partnership, has on relationships with the other "partner." The individual missionary's lifestyle, and style of ministry, conveys its own message—a message that may contradict kingdom values.

In contrast to the affluent Western missionary, Third World missionaries conduct "mission out of poverty." It can be truly said of him or her, "as poor, yet making many rich; as having nothing, and yet possessing everything" (2 Cor. 6:10). Being have-nots themselves, Asian, African, or Latin American missionaries identify easily with other have-nots. The experience they gain in the years immediately ahead may be instructive to Western missionaries.

According to Theodore Williams, the Indian leader mentioned earlier, another contribution that emerging missions can make to Western missionaries is their emphasis on the servant role. "Bereft of all political status and national glory the missionary from the Third World can truly be the servant of all," he notes. Most Western missionaries, Williams contends, are success-orientated and number-conscious; they are given over to a certain missiological triumphalism. Mission, Williams says, should be carried out "in the servant image, not in the domineering, aggressive posture of some Western evangelists. The people of India have scant respect for the activist, busy-body image. . . . It is not the fulfillment of programmes but the fulfilling of human relationships that matter. If we ride roughshod over the feelings of people and have no time for individuals, under the guise of carrying out projects and programmes for God, our mission has no credibility."[9] This Indian friend speaks frankly. Are we able to hear?

Along with their capacity for sacrifice and service, Third World missionaries bring a renewed emphasis on suffering. In many countries of Asia and Africa, Christians are a minority group, persecuted and oppressed. Suffering is part of their mission. The cross is an ever present reality. Knowing this, it seems imperative that the missionaries we send out from the West be committed to the kind of lifestyle and ministry that will enable them to become true partners with their fellow Christians in the Third World.

Training

The poor are the world's majority. In the United States, however, they are a minority. Therefore prospective American missionaries will benefit most by that kind of training that immerses them in minority groups in American society. Here they may experience in microcosm the special problems and aspirations of the vast majority of the world's population. A summer in Harlem, or with migrant workers in California, or on a Navajo reservation will bring to life the lessons of the seminary classroom in a way suburbia never can. It is a pity that so few of these minority-oriented training programs are a structural part of our missionary preparation. Perhaps short terms abroad are more exotic.

Ultimately, however, any discussion of missionary preparation will focus on congregational life. Most missionaries are nurtured for considerable lengths of time within the local congregation. The attitudes, convictions, and lifestyle of the missionary are likely to mirror those of his or her home congregation. Are our churches in solidarity with the weak and powerless? Or are we in reality committed to the very forces in society that exploit and oppress? It is reasonable to expect that a congregation that evaluates its contextual role critically and moves unitedly toward the poor at the margins of life will provide the environment in which the missionaries of tomorrow will flourish.

NOTES

1. A "people" is defined as a significantly large sociological grouping of individuals who perceive themselves as having a common affinity for one another.

2. Editorial, *International Review of Mission* 68, no. 270 (April 1979): 100.

3. Cf. Mahbub ul Haq, *The Poverty Curtain* (New York: Columbia University Press, 1976).

4. Cf. Michael Harrington's *The Vast Majority* (New York: Simon and Schuster, 1977). According to the *1979 World Bank Atlas,* the average gross national product (GNP) per capita for 70 percent of the world's population is $1,000 or less.

5. "Third World" is a shorthand phrase for much of Asia, Africa, and Latin America. The phrase is not altogether acceptable and I use it sparingly.

6. See my book, *Bring Forth Justice* (Grand Rapids, Mich.: Eerdmans, 1980).

7. The East-West pairing reflects cultural differences dominant in our thinking over many centuries. More recently, political and economic differences are seen to be of greater urgency. This is reflected in the North-South pairing, where the North represents the industrialized world and the South the developing countries.

8. Theodore Williams, "Bridges in Mission," in Waldron Scott, ed., *Serving Our Generation: Evangelical Strategies for the Eighties* (Colorado Springs: World Evangelical Fellowship, 1980), pp. 127ff.

9. Theodore Williams, "The Servant Image," *AIM* (September 1980), p. 20.

Congregational Renewal
for Mission and Evangelism
in the United States of America

WILLIAM H. HANNAH

My task is to look through the experience of the Conference on World Mission and Evangelism at Melbourne and to draw out several of the significant issues and apply them to the North American scene. How can these issues be related to congregational renewal and evangelism in the United States? We are speaking of congregational renewal in the sense of the reawakening of persons in congregations to the evangelistic task of the church, so that they may serve as a cadre to witness and lead those outside the community of faith to a living experience with Christ. It is believed by many contemporary church leaders that when persons and congregations are inspired by the Word, motivated by the Spirit and a revisioning of God's good news, renewal is in process. During the process of renewal, persons will be motivated by the Holy Spirit to witness in a powerful way to God's good news in word and deed. It is at that point that the Christian's concern will not only be about the salvation of other persons, but a constant and consistent care of and for all persons.

Under the theme "Your Kingdom Come" several hundred persons of many nations, countries, and languages gathered for two weeks at Melbourne to discuss the meaning of the theme and the Lord's Prayer as a whole for the universal church. While the conference had a tendency to drift into abstraction as some of the more theologically astute persons were able to demand exegetical jots and tittles, there was always an urgency expressed by the representatives of the poor, the oppressed, and the alienated persons in the world. There was a sense of urgency to move on to some suggested plan for Christian involvement and resolution of the world's human problems. There was a mournful, heart-wrenching cry of the powerless to the powerful of the world—a cry of despair and hope. It was a cry that offered new opportunities and challenges for the church to experience the kerygma, the didache, the koinonia and diakonia. The conference offered a stage to demonstrate the human plight in the light and context of Matthew 6:9–13, the Lord's Prayer. This became an opportunity to see graphically a worldview of the church and the opportunities for witnessing to the kingdom.

One of the most significant implications for renewal and evangelism in our contemporary society is wrapped up in the prayer recorded in Matthew's Gospel, which we studied in small groups at the conference. These Bible reflections were not only opportunities to sit under the Word, but always challenged the participants to seek ways of authenticating the Word by the deed.

The church in the United States would do well to reconsider the issue of this prayer as it responds to the call and task of evangelism and renewal. The issue of Christian credibility surfaced repeatedly as the representatives from the socially and economically deprived nations accused the powerful and affluent nations of default in terms of sharing God's abundance, of promises not delivered, and of exploitation in a myriad of ways. The question was how we can believe in a gospel of good news when those who proclaim the good news often seem to join and protect the forces of bad news. How long will the church cover up its prophetic role by involvement in busy service or maintenance activities? This issue of credibility continues to confront the institutional church. What will the church in the United States say and do in a society that "eats up persons" and becomes more depersonalized and exploitative of the poor, people of color, and women?

Then there is the issue of how congregations will utilize new awareness and consciousness of evangelism as it relates to the heart of the mission of the church. How can a congregation put into practice the communication of God's good news?

While the Melbourne Conference raised many challenges and issues for the universal church, three issues in particular are vital for our consideration: (1) the significance of the Lord's Prayer in Matthew's Gospel for congregational renewal and evangelism;

(2) the credibility of the church among the poor, the oppressed, and the exploited; (3) communication for congregational renewal and evangelism.

The Significance of the Lord's Prayer in Matthew's Gospel for Congregational Renewal and Evangelism

The prayer sets some basic parameters for renewal and evangelism. It begins with God the creator, and the relationship with the created, a family relationship implying love and care. It is clear that all peoples of the world are brothers and sisters, all are in God's family. In many ways the prayer points up the fallacy of ever acting on the false notion that one group of persons is better than another group of persons. Any racist notion that one race is better than another is utterly unbiblical.

If evangelism and renewal are going to take place in the North American scene, the issue of race must be put behind us. The sinful deification of white skin must cease. The Lord's Prayer calls all Christians to acknowledge that blacks, browns, reds, yellows, whites, and all shades of people in between are children of God and belong to the family of God. Those who insist on the superiority-inferiority status for certain people are accusing God of having illegitimate children; they are saying that everything which God created was not and is not good, that God made a mistake and made white-skinned people more valuable and superior to people of other colors.

The prayer affirms the fatherhood of God and the family of God. The task of evangelism and renewal is to help Christians to relearn the lesson of a common father who loves and cares for all of his children. Some of the children are estranged from the family for one reason or another, some have gone into a far country trying to find self and meaning for life; some have given up because everything seems hopeless, the rich get richer, the poor get poorer. People are oppressed because they belong to certain cultures and races and speak different languages.

Those who are in loving relationship with the Father through Jesus Christ are to go wherever necessary to reclaim the alienated brothers and sisters and restore them to the family through love and reconciliation. This is not always an easy chore but it must be done because the family of God is never complete as long as there are individuals acting as though they are not members of the family. "Our Father" is not only the beginning of a model prayer, but a fact. This fact serves as a launching place for those that would experience congregational renewal and evangelism. The Father not only cares, but he prepares individuals through his son, Jesus Christ, and empowers them through the Holy Spirit to be faithful in their involvement in the task of evangelism.

The Father saw the hopeless alienation of his children. He sent his son as mediator, advocate, and savior, to serve as a bridge between the children and the Father. The Father's heart grieved for his children: "He was not willing that any be lost." Jesus came from the Father not to point the way to the Father but actually to be the way for reconciliation with the Father. The Father is so loving that he welcomes all of his children from the far country with open arms. When this message of love and care is internalized and becomes incarnate in the lives of persons and congregations, spiritual renewal will take place in a radical and dynamic way. Persons and congregations will be literally propelled into communities all over the country, loving, caring, and sharing God's good news. In essence that good news is an invitation to all persons outside the community of faith—all persons that are alienated from the Father and the family. God the Father is willing and waiting for each person to accept his Son's invitation to come back to the family. The prayer also implies an attitude of humility and trust. It serves as a spiritual conduit between the children and the Father. It dramatizes in a unique way the accessibility of the Father for the children. That accessibility of the Father for the children ensures the divine presence and power to encourage and enlighten the children to be in relationship with the Father and with each other.

The problem that most congregations experience in doing evangelism is the problem of spiritual maintenance. Many groups begin with enthusiasm and power, but lose their passion for evangelism. It is absolutely essential that a disciplined prayer life be developed and maintained. Prayer is the conduit for the Holy Spirit to provide power and passion for the task of evangelism.

Congregational worship can be the vehicle for maintaining the vision of power to remain at the task of doing evangelism in word and deed. Renewal and evangelism are inextricably bound together and will almost always act in concert for faithfulness and obedience in witnessing to the kingdom. In this context evangelism and renewal occur with integrity and authenticity.

The Credibility of the Church among the Poor, the Oppressed, and the Exploited

It is difficult for the average North American church person to understand why the church has so little credibility among the poor and oppressed and exploited in America. Jesus was biased toward poor people. His first public statement at the beginning of his earthly ministry witnesses to his concern for the poor: "The Spirit of the Lord is upon me, because he has anointed me to preach good news to the poor . . ." (Lk. 4:18). Congregations that have decided on the principle of homogeneity and the notion of postponing social awareness have been able to attract many persons to their membership, but they lose credibility with a large segment of society—a segment that was of vital interest to Jesus. Historically the church has too often been associated with the oppression and exploitation of the poor. Churches have been identified with the involuntary servitude of blacks and the exploitation of migrant workers. In the 1960s, however, the church began to shake itself from its institutional self-preservation and for awhile became prophetic. In the prophetic leadership of Martin Luther King, Jr., the church in America had its finest hour. Civil rights bills were passed, and great promises were made by the federal government. After James Forman's "Black Manifesto," some churches confessed their guilt and made promises to the exploited and oppressed, the blacks, and the poor in America. In the 1980s, however, conditions for all minorities have deteriorated *even worse* than before all the marches and demonstrations in the 1960s.

The 1954 Supreme Court School Desegregation Order has not been fully implemented. Unemployment is much higher among blacks and browns than whites. There is a resurgence of the Ku Klux Klan and other hate groups. There is a serious swing to the right politically and religiously. American church persons are indeed surprised when they learn that they have very little credibility among the poor, the oppressed, and the expoited.

It is not too late for the church, however, to be obedient to God in Christ. Credibility will come when the church decides to lose itself. When it moves from a maintenance-survival syndrome to a posture of mission that has at its heart renewal and evangelism; when the church decides to call for and stand for justice; when the church decides to give its allegiance, its power, and its love to God before it gives it to America; when the church recognizes its new role as an advocate for the poor, the oppressed, and the exploited —only then will credibility be established.

The theme "Your Kingdom Come" offers further instruction for the family of God. It is a petition for the reign and rule of God in the hearts of persons, so that they can witness to the kingdom by proclaiming God's good news to all persons regardless of social status. The coming of the kingdom can be the impetus for changing greed, arrogance, and violence to love and care for the whole human family of God. The poor, the oppressed, and the exploited are not overly impressed with periodic manifestations of the church's commitment to the kingdom, although there is always hope that the kingdom will indeed come on earth as it is in heaven. The cry is "How long?" Among the marginalized people in our society there is a suspicion that the church continues to subscribe to the principles of homogeneity and the postponement of social awareness. Many church persons feel less threatened with this kind of attitude. Many other persons in our society, however, are waiting on the church to be prophetic and to be an agent of healing. The question remains "How long?" Credibility for the church will continue to be under serious scrutiny by persons outside the community of faith until the church begins to lose itself for those who are injured, the dying, the separated of the world.

Communication for Congregational Renewal and Evangelism

Most mainline denominations have developed evangelism resources in the past few years in trying to meet the needs and requests from their particular constituency. However, there is very little evidence to document a wide use of available evangelism materials describing various evangelism methodologies. There are many national and international conferences on evangelism, but little evidence that the results of these conferences are effectively communicated to congregations.

In the case of the Melbourne Conference, how can the participants communicate the tensions, the fears, the hopes, and the dreams of that conference to their churches at home? Denominational representatives will need to put forth an extra effort to communicate with their constituency concerning the need to proclaim God's good news in word and deed. There are many congregations in North America that do not have the denominational structure to implement a program of communication, especially to ethnic minority congregations.

Basically the question remains concerning what kind of methodology can be developed and used to communicate intentionally with a majority of congregations in North America concerning crucial issues involved in motivating persons to take seriously the task of evangelism. Several things can be done in this area. Ecumenical groups will develop a program to challenge congregations concerning holistic evangelism, and will develop and implement regular skill-enhancing events. Congregations can organize small discussion groups to consider *what is the purpose of the congregation,* using the Bible as a resource for discussion and reflection.

Communication must occur from the sender to the receiver and from the receiver to the sender. Congregations will not make progress toward renewal or evangelism unless they decide *as a congregation,* and not leave it to the evangelism committee. When the congregation decides, studies, plans, works, and prays for congregational renewal, it will happen. Communication will take place in congregations and among persons when the good news grips their lives in a heart-warming way, but the heart not will be satisfied until that good news has been shared with others in a relational way.

Congregations of all sizes and beliefs have the responsibility to form clusters and partnerships in order to communicate current information concerning the task of evangelism. Persons inside the community of faith must learn how to communicate with each other as well as how to communicate with those outside the community of faith, in witnessing to the kingdom. When this is done effectively, God's kingdom will indeed come.

Ecumenism from 1960 into the 1980s: A Roman Catholic View of Melbourne

THOMAS F. STRANSKY, C.S.P.

Only two weeks after the exhausted yet exhilarated six hundred participants from one hundred countries left the Melbourne Conference, this departing observer could rejoice in the twentieth anniversary of Pope John XXIII's creation of the Secretariat for Promoting Christian Unity (June 5, 1960). With two decades of easy hindsight, one now sees that papal act as the official positive entrance of the Roman Catholic church into that single ecumenical movement, wherein each Christian communion is equally called to contribute, according to its conscience, whatever can restore the full invisible and visible unity Christ wills for his body-in-mission. "Whatever can" took on the flesh of a charter four years later. In that lengthy examination of conscience that was Vatican Council II (1962–65), over two thousand bishops approved the Decree on Ecumenism (*Unitatis Redintegratio,* Nov. 21, 1964).

The focus of the council, one recalls, was *renewal,* renewal in all personal and communal aspects of the internal and external life of the church, "an increase of fidelity to her [the Church's] own calling" (Decree, no. 6, hereafter references only by division numbers).[1]

Already the first paragraph of the decree offers a missionary motive for ecumenical involvement. The present division among Christians "contradicts the will of Christ, provides a stumbling block to the world, and damages that most holy cause, the proclamation of the Gospel to every creature." Nevertheless, because of the Christ-given bonds that already unite Christians in a real but imperfect communion, their cooperation in mission "sets in clearer relief the features of Christ the Servant" (no. 12).

Not a peculiar, original Roman Catholic insight. I can testify that the drafting of the decree, as well as of similar ecumenical/missionary expressions in the other fifteen council documents, was influenced by that deepening conviction that already had led in 1961 to the integration of the International Missionary Council with the World Council of Churches, and thus to the formation of the Commission on World Mission and Evangelism: in God's will for his church, mission, unity, and renewal are integral and inseparable. Fifteen years after Vatican II, Christian consensus affirms that the most acceptable, overarching biblical paradigm of God's building up the kingdom through that portion of humankind called church is unity-in-mission, mission-in-unity. *Ecumenism means unity for mission through personal, communal, and church renewal*: the obligation to draw all Christians into one renewed church always in renewal; and the obligation of the whole church to proclaim, by word or act, the whole gospel in and to the whole world, as sacramental herald and servant to both that gospel and that world. The slogan is "holistic mission"—not to separate what God already holds together.

At Melbourne this paradigm was presumed. It rested in the top drawer of the participants' minds rather than being monotonously proclaimed. Yet there was a strong, explicit affirmation: "we believe that unless the pilgrimage route leads the churches to visible unity, in the one God we preach and worship, the one Christ crucified for us all, the one Holy Spirit who creates us anew, and the one kingdom, the mission entrusted to us in this world will always be rightly questioned" (Section III, 24).

Furthermore, during the past fifteen years there has emerged a working principle that derives from the accepted fact that the whole of humankind is now sharing a single, interrelated secular and religious history. The principle: *just as a worldwide ecumenical/missionary vision is unreal if it is not also local, so the local vision—no matter how local—is unreal if it is not also worldwide*. By biblical demand and now historical definition, the real vision of mission-in-unity and unity-in-mission is bifocal. So "bifocal vision" joins other familiar slogans: "global village," "mission in and to six continents," "two-way traffic" or "a local church matures as it learns equally to give and receive from other local churches," "partnership in mission," "local context in world context, vice versa," and so forth. At Melbourne all these expressions were heard in conference hall and seminar class-rooms.

Such a broadly representative gathering as at Melbourne indicates more where the constituency *is* and *wants to be* than where a specialist claims it should be. Melbourne indicated what ecumenical/missionary currents are flowing in the churches, even though there are different strengths and paces in the flow. The fact that Melbourne so naturally accepted both that biblical para-digm (unity-in-mission, mission-in-unity) and that working prin-ciple (bifocal vision) indicates gigantic strides of Christian con-sciousness in two decades. One can see similar streams also in Roman Catholic meetings; for example, at the triennial Bishops' Synods in Rome, especially those of 1971 ("Justice in the World"), 1974 ("Evangelization"), and 1977 ("Catechetics"). I add, however, that such synods indicate where only Roman Catholic episcopal representatives stand. No worldwide cross-section of Roman Catholics (bishops, clergy, and laity from six continents) has ever assembled. One cannot accurately read the Roman Catholic pulse on marriage and family life by evaluating only what the bishops proclaimed at the 1980 Synod. The topic is indeed both missionary and ecumenical!

Also in evaluating any such international meeting, one should keep eagle eyes open to the ways in which the triplets—mission, unity, renewal—are understood and applied. In the light of what Melbourne reflected, much in these three areas has happened in and to the churches since Vatican Council II. These developments evoke a radical shift in ecumenical/missionary thinking and prac-tices. The churches should acknowledge and pursue this shift, so that in the remaining decades of our millennium they can achieve realistic, authentic progress in ecumenism.

I can best illustrate this thesis by looking again at the 1964 De-cree on Ecumenism and by pointing therein to those ecumenical developments that were accurately projected for the immediate future and, more important, those three that were *not* adequately foreseen, and perhaps could not have been anticipated, at least their speed. Since the decree was a more boldly comprehensive, forward-looking schematic attempt than those few efforts from other churches and interdenominational groups in the early

1960s, one should not judge the decree as singularly myopic. That council act humbly concludes with the firm hope that "the initiatives of the sons [*sic*] of the Catholic Church, joined with those of the separated brethren, go forward without obstructing the ways of divine Providence, and without prejudging the future inspirations of the Holy Spirit" (no. 24).

These three unanticipated developments are: (1) the weakening of the classical typology of Christian divisions (East/West and Intra-West) by the rapid emergence of the Third Church (Asia/Oceania/Latin America/Africa), bonded together by poverty; (2) the breaking up of intact confessional traditions by the emergence of new fluid ones, especially in the Third Church; (3) the shifting of mission power clusters by the rapid, influential growth of the Evangelicals.

Vatican II classified historically "the two principal types of division which affect the seamless robe of Christ": the gradual dissolving of ecclesiastical communion between the Patriarchates of the East and the Roman See in the West; and within the West four centuries later, between the Roman See and the national or confessional churches issuing from the Reformation (cf. no. 13). These divided Western churches later parented almost all the infant communities in Asia, Africa, Latin America, and Oceania. Following this typology of Christian divisions and their Western exportations, the decree implies that theological dialogues and pastoral solicitude should concentrate on the healing of both East/West and Intra-West divisions, and so, one hopes, could come about the unity of the renewed and renewing church and the integrity of its mission *everywhere*.

I

To be specific, I outline the Decree's program. On the local, national, regional, and international levels, bilateral and multilateral dialogues, engaged in by historians, cultural sociologists, theologians, and others, should concentrate on the classical priority hotspots. With the Eastern churches these are apostolic origins, apostolic succession, and the bishop of Rome (cf. no. 14); the diversity of liturgies, religious customs, spiritualities and disciplines (cf. nos. 15–16); and the "legitimate variety" of complementary theological expressions of doctrine (cf. no. 17). Between the divided Western churches the disputed themes are Christ's work of redemption and the mystery and ministry of the church (cf. no. 20); the relationship between Scripture, Tradition, and traditions, and the church's teaching office (cf. no. 21); "the true meaning of the Lord's Supper [and] the other sacraments " (no. 22); and "the application of the gospel to moral questions" (no. 23).

What fifteen years ago was not foreseen is the new and growing tension between this classical, still somewhat but no longer exclusive legitimate typology of Christian divisions with its agenda, and the rapidly growing "Third Church," to use Walbert Bühlmann's phrase. The traditional center that embraced the local churches of the Northern Atlantic/Eastern European/ Mediterranean areas is fading in its dominant influence over those centers that are no longer mere passive recipients of the southern hemisphere—Latin America, Africa, Asia, and Oceania. As both a geographical and a historical repositioning, these areas are becoming the new centers of theological articulations, personal and social ethical stances, spiritualities, church disciplines, artistic expressions, interchurch cooperation, and structural forms of "home" and "foreign" missions. Even the quantitative center of gravity is moving rapidly; by conservative estimates of growth patterns, by the year 2000 from 55 to 60 percent of all Christians (70 percent of all Catholics) will be living outside North America and Europe.

During the past two decades, the local Western churches, including their overseas mission groups, were replacing euphoric self-confidence with missionary discouragement, doubt, and masochistic guilt—and as a result, overall fatigue and out of that fatigue either defensiveness or cynicism. But during the same period, the Third Church was witnessing to a new dynamism, self-confidence, and a strong will of finding its own way into tomorrow's world, especially within the new nations of Africa and Asia. The 1970s saw in Europe/North America a standstill or decline in committed church membership, except for the "conservative Evangelicals"; while in other parts of the world there was a noticeable increase, and not only through the cradle.

At Melbourne one saw this realignment of influence, as well as a shifting psychological mood. Those from the North, no longer a majority voice or wanting to be, were less nervous and more humbly self-assured about their missionary responsibility to their own and cross-cultural/national milieux. Those from the South, the Third Church, are unembarrassingly articulate (especially the Latin Americans). They possess a chastened, more mature and realistic self-confidence. In fact, strident strains came from those at Melbourne who seemed to have borrowed the iconoclastic language of recent Western vintage in speaking about "the church" (are they not of it?). Too much of that sour wine seeped into the final documents.

If the churches of the southern hemisphere recognize a shared identity in all three continents, it is the mark of poverty and dependency—"the development of underdevelopment." Their general cry was voiced, heard, and acknowledged by the Melbourne participants. Ahead of all Melbourne's other forward steps, it showed that Christian communities more and more consciously believe that the body of Christ is called to be the church *with, for,* and above all, *of* the poor. No matter how debates run on the biblical categories of poverty and their causes, those fellow human beings, as both sinners and sinned-against, call out in Christ's name for justice and love. And the poor are not confined to the South. As a descriptive term, *Third World* is now shifting away from geography to an emerging consciousness of that part of the deprived and relatively powerless people wherever they exist or subexist. Furthermore, they are called to take their destiny into their own hands, to become the "subject" and no longer the passive "object" of a history determined by others. Thus the biblically poor are also the bearers and agents of mission, not just its objects. "World mission and evangelism must now be primarily in their hands" (Section IV, 21).

The discovery of the poor is a rediscovery of the gospel, indeed a rediscovery of the very identity of the church. *The* question for all the churches everywhere in the decades ahead is: How much will this faith-conviction shape the criteria by which one should evaluate the success or failure of the mission/unity/renewal triad, or should judge the authenticity and credibility of the church?

II

A second oversight in the decree is related. In 1964 that ecumenical charter stressed "unity in essentials," with a "proper freedom in the various forms of spiritual life and discipline, in the variety of liturgical rites, and even in the theological elaborations of revealed truth" (no. 4). Nevertheless, one presupposed continuing *intact* theological and ecclesiastical traditions. These would merge when, in the common search, "the essentials" would be happily discovered and "the unessentials" acknowledged and respected. In fifteen years of dialogues, confessional frontiers have indeed tended to shade off, even on such formerly divisive issues as baptism, Eucharist, and ministry, or the debate on the Bible and its authoritative interpretation through a historical community. The process must go on.

But along with this dialogue between presupposed intact confessional traditions has been the sudden emergence of new fluid ones. Now we are more conscious of the dialectic between traditional biblical and limited historical understandings, and the new, changing, and different contexts of common witness to the hope that is in us (cf. 1 Pet. 3:5) by selfless reconciling service to humankind. Again the dominant new contexts are in the Third Church arenas.

The pressure has led, for example, to the formation in 1976 of the Ecumenical Association of Third World Theologians (EATWOT). These leaders agree on at least three premises: (1) they can no longer with integrity be passive recipients of North American/European theologies; (2) they cannot accept without question the ecumenical agenda based on the classical typologies of Christian divisions ("East or West, it's still North!"), or the method of establishing such agendas, or the conclusions passed on for everybody's consumption; and (3) they cannot continue monotonously to chant that the theological enterprise must be "de-Westernized" or "de-imperialized"—this is a question of method; they themselves must begin to do theology; but it is a question of method *and* content. So the beginnings of this new theologizing, led in Asia by M. M. Thomas, Samuel Rayan, Raymond Fung, Choan-Seng Song, Kosuke Koyama, C. Duraisingh, S. Wesley Ariarajah, and Stanley Samartha; in Africa by John Mbiti, K. A. Dickson, E. Fasholé-Luke, John Pobee, and Peter Sarpong; in Latin America by Gustavo Gutiérrez, Juan Segundo, José Miguez-Bonino, Jon Sobrino, and Rubem Alves. These people, among others, are having more than a restricted academic influence within the WCC forum.

Their consensus represents a constituency much larger than EATWOT. Many of them were at Melbourne. True, it was not a gathering only of biblical scholars and professional theologians but more a cross section of church folk. Yet such folk did have words to say about God and the world and the church. These "Melbourne theologies," these reflections and experiences in the light of God's Word, show that if one can generalize the Third Church by poverty and dependency, one observes also the wide differences of theological reflection within this general Christian context by looking at the participants from Latin America, then Africa, then Asia.

Within both WCC and Roman Catholic circles, Latin Americans propagate the method of *praxis,* an unending reciprocity between action and reflection within a community of God's self-disclosure through yearnings and hopes, pains and uncertainties, and through loving and liberating actions. Theology is not a head-trip of "endless prologemena *about* a liberation that never takes place" (P. Hebblethwaite). Theology is *for* liberation. One understands faith through an act of solidarity with the humiliated poor, and such an act calls forth a political commitment to change society. If the results disturb "the wise according to this world," so much the better. "Liberation" always points an accusing finger.

Latin Americans speak militantly, as they did at Melbourne, in the context of exploitation and institutionalized violence. But their context is also traditionally Christian. In their proclamation and action, they emphasize commitment to the liberating Christ as a national and continental concern. They rightly stress the actual and potential clout of the large institutional church, especially through its increasing solidarity of the basic communities of prayer, study, and social service *(comunidades de base)*. In many ways this is a Christian variation of a Western situation and response—a primary reason, I suspect, why of all three continents of the South, Latin American liberation theologies are avidly understood, debated, and to some extent being integrated into, say, North American theological, missionary, and pastoral discourse.

Black African contexts and reflection thereon are quite different from the Latin American. The agenda in Africa concerns the interpretation and translation of God's self-disclosure in Christian contacts with traditional mythologies, ethics, and rituals; the biblical revelation on such themes as eschatology, communion of saints, healing; family ethical issues such as customary marriage, polygamy, the unmarried life, and divorce; the trialogue between Christianity, traditional religions, and Islam; and a political theology of development, nation-building, church-and-state.

The Asians at Melbourne, self-admittedly rarely loud or persistent, quietly let it be known that their situation should not be lumped together with all other struggles and deprivations. Nor do they identify with that model and method of liberation which Latin Americans are proposing, "because the liberation we [Asians] must have is from *our* captivities, and for such liberation we need other perspectives and other sensitivities." In this stubborn concern over Asian contexts, one sees theologies developing that could be radically different from those emerging out of the African and Latin American contexts.

With four centuries of missionary presence, Asian Christians remain an insignificant minority: a mere 2 percent of the masses. Even here a good half of this 2 percent is in the Philippines, which, in its process of becoming Christian, had been forced to cut off its Asian roots—a magnified version of most Christian communities scattered throughout the Asian diaspora. Fully 95 percent of Asia has no meaningful contact with Christians.

The specific character that defines Asia with the other poor countries of the South is its multifaceted religiosity. In the cultural ethos of Asia, poverty and religiosity coalesce to procreate the Asian character. Theological attempts to encounter Asian religions with no radical concern for the poor, and ideological programs to eradicate the poverty with naive disregard for Asian religiosity have both proved to be misdirected zeal. Asian Christian leaders are quite aware of avoiding the trap.

Furthermore, Asian Christian culture is called to relate to the ancient traditions, which over five thousand years have evolved coherent answers to the problems of human existence. And the resurgence of religions in Asia—Islam and Hinduism, Shintoism and Buddhism—is the overall context within which this small Christian minority must give witness to Christ through a community life that is often precarious.

This situation provides the opportunity for creative modes of Christian presence by humble participation in the non-Christian experiences of liberation—for example, with Buddhism, which may be the one religion that is pan-Asian in cultural integration, numerical strength, and political maturity. Yes, how is the kingdom of Jesus the Lord to be faithfully proclaimed in Asia?

In short, the Third Church boasts of vastly different contexts, which are pressuring the churches into a whole new range of shared reflections and common witness. Thereby they are already creating new but fluid ecumenical traditions, which do not fit the classical categories of Christian historical and theological divisions, and which are breaking up the imported intact confessional traditions.

Furthermore, bonded together by poverty and institutionalized dependency, the South asks Roman Catholics, Protestants, and Orthodox to look afresh at the classical ecumenical agenda: the Bible of Yahweh who sees the affliction of his people, knows their suffering, and intends to deliver them (cf. Exod. 3:7–8); Christ's redemption in the historical struggles of today; Christ's ministry and our ministries in the church of reconciliation (cf. 2 Cor. 5:18), of breaking down hostile walls between peoples (cf. Eph. 2:14); and the structures and exercise of a teaching authority that proclaims God's "just deeds" in the translation of the love of God into the doing of justice.

A pronounced example of this same-agenda-but-new-context is Melbourne's reflection on the Eucharist "as a witness to the Kingdom of God and an experience of God's reign" (Section III, 28–31). Though not the well-honed conclusions of a Faith and Order conference of academic theologians, the statement is not only a miracle of the recent dialogues and their gradual reception among the churches. For this Roman Catholic, that statement was also the one most challenging to future mission theology, spirituality, and practice. It holds together personal and communal discipleship in "the true rhythm of Christian engagement in the world": "gathering *and* dispersing, receiving *and* giving, praise *and* work, prayer *and* struggle" through social action. The Eucharist is pilgrim bread, missionary bread.

If there are any danger flags gently waving, they are hinting that the bifocal vision be not impaired. "Contextual theologies," no matter what their varieties, still have the theater of God's whole world as part of the context. This corrects any parochialism that can easily produce its own heresies or illegitimate isolations. And at the same time, the "northern theologies" do not have the privileged position of primary judge before whom Latin American, African, Asian ones must play court and justify themselves. In fact, the Western churches should increase and sustain their attention to "contextualize" the gospel at home. Lesslie Newbigin has suggested that "the most pressing missiological issue for the coming years" is how the Western church can become the bearer of God's Word of grace and judgment, heard as relevant yet challenging Western worldviews. This former bishop in India hopes that "the great work that has been done during the last decade in exploring the meaning of contextualization in relation to non-western cultures may, in the decade now beginning, enable us to undertake with comparable energy and seriousness the exploration of the problem of contextualization in relation to the powerful paganism of our own Western world." Melbourne does not leave the North off the hook.

III

There has been yet another unanticipated development within the Christian Family-in-mission in the last fifteen years. Catholic scholars who have been competently engaging in a whole series of local, national, and world bilateral and multilateral dialogues are now realizing that their partners are restricted to the Anglican and Protestant traditions, with mainline scholastic variations. And at the very time when many surveyors were predicting the death of much denominationalism and seeing new alignments and clusters forming within the emerging church of the future, a large Christian segment was rapidly growing in numbers and influence. What the 1964 decree did not clearly envisage was the extent of the present cleavage between the mainstream Protestants/Orthodox/ Roman Catholics, and the commonly called Conservative Evangelicals. A few weeks after the World Mission and Evangelism Conference at Melbourne, another equally large international mission consultation was convened by the Lausanne Committee for World Evangelization at Pattaya, Thailand.

The constituencies of both meetings defy simple categories of radical contrast. But in the light of the two conferences, too many Evangelicals seem to downplay, in practice if not in theory, the mission struggle for just, sustainable, and participatory societies in a world divided between the haves and have-nots. And too many of the Melbourne people seem to downplay, at least in practice, explicit evangelism among those millions of "unreached," not yet graced by explicit faith and discipleship. One should add that many Evangelical descriptions of those "beyond the frontiers of the Gospel" include other Christians; and that some methods of evangelizing these "nominals" are questioned, if not downright condemned in the ecumenical arena.

Melbourne and Pattaya explicitly profess their common commitment to the whole gospel of the whole church for the whole world. But for this observer at both meetings, too many look warily at each with judgmental coldness: "the gospel salt has lost its savor among those others." I suspect that the wider Melbourne and Pattaya constituencies form a too silent majority; they would reject such reciprocal caricatures, and refuse to take sides. A growing number of Evangelicals, "conciliar, ecumenical" Anglicans, Protestants, Roman Catholics, and Orthodox worry about this artificial structuring of world mission in the stewardship of precious personnel, funds, and energies. At Melbourne many, including Emilio Castro of the CWME, lamented the insufficient attention given to "primary evangelism"—reaching the unreached, whether within or across cultural frontiers. Also at Pattaya, a goodly number who were zealously concerned in offering a valid opportunity to all unreached peoples to be challenged by good news were, through a formal written plea, equally concerned that the overwhelming majority of these unreached peoples are "the powerless and oppressed of the earth": "The God of the Gospel not only speaks (Heb. 1:1) but sees the condition of the oppressed (Ex. 2:35) and hears their cry (Ex. 3:7; Jas. 5:1-5; Acts

7:34). Jesus himself sets the example of an authentic evangelization by proclaiming the Gospel to the poor in word and deed (Mt. 11:4–6)."

Conclusion

At the 1980 plenary meeting of the bishop members and consultors of the Secretariat for Promoting Christian Unity, Pope John Paul II pressed Christians to bear common witness, "straightaway and wherever possible," to "the gifts of faith and life that they have received from God," a "true witness to the Gospel, borne to Jesus Christ living in the fullness of the Church today." But, regrets the pope, this common witness now is still "limited and imcomplete as long as we disagree about the content of the faith we have to proclaim. Hence, the importance of unity for evangelization."[2]

In the light of the developments in and between all churches and mission groups touched upon in this chapter, these familiar expressions of gospel demands, now echoed by a pope, are filling up with new interpretations about "the content of faith." Because we are called to "fill up what is wanting" in Christ's faith by faithfulness to our own times, then one concludes, with bifocal vision, by rephrasing the question: What is the fulfillment of the triadic mission/unity/renewal of the church, called to be with, for, and of the poor, in and to six continents?

NOTES

1. Quotations from *Decree on Ecumenism* are from the translation by John Long, S.J. and Thomas F. Stransky, C.S.P. (New York: Paulist Press, 1965).

2. *L'Osservatore Romano,* Feb. 9, 1980.

On Orthodox Witness

MICHAEL OLEKSA

If we could travel today along the route the disciples followed in their missionary journeys, "beginning at Jerusalem," we would discover in each populated city and village Orthodox Christian churches, founded by the original apostles of Jesus Christ. We would find also the tombs of hundreds of martyrs who suffered for the faith during ancient Roman persecutions, and of other martyrs who died during Arab, Persian, or Turkish oppression because of their determination to live and preach the gospel. For most of twenty centuries, the Eastern Christians have lived under extremely difficult political conditions. This persecution has welded them into a committed and easily identifiable community, like the "Old Israel," on one hand, but has seriously limited the freedom of the Orthodox to evangelize new territories. Whenever the Eastern church was free to send missions to non-Christian nations, however, they were quite successful in converting "pagan" tribes to Christ. In the ninth century Greek missionaries translated the Scriptures into Slavonic for the people of Eastern Europe, and brought Christianity to the Serbs, Bulgars, Moravians, and Russians, who in turn evangelized dozens of Central Asian and North American tribes during the next nine hundred years. The tremendous missionary work of the Eastern churches has hardly been recognized in the West because for nearly one thousand years the two "halves" of Christendom have had very little contact with each other.

Since World War I much of this has changed. Millions of Southern and Eastern European and Middle Eastern Christians have left their traditionally Orthodox countries in search of religious and political liberty in the West. After nearly ten centuries of oppression and isolation the Eastern Orthodox church has become a "fact" of religious life in the West, especially in America. This represents a great opportunity for the Orthodox to witness to their ancient faith in a free country, and for Christians, separated for so long, to get acquainted at last.

Getting Acquainted

For the first thousand years A.D. the Christian church was undivided. (It is true that in the sixth century there was a major "split" over some theological terms, but modern ecumenical discussions have shown that this division was a misunderstanding aggravated by the "international politics" of the time.) There was one visible community to which all Christians belonged. They shared the same doctrines, the same sacraments, the same "style" of worship. Because there was such complete unity, these first centuries are for the Orthodox the most important period in Christian history. The Orthodox believe that the church *must* be united, *must* be "one," and not two or six or three hundred (cf. Mt. 16:18; Jn. 17:21). This oneness is not created by human beings, but *given* by God. Because we are sinful and limited in our wisdom and intelligence, people are prone to disagree, as church history itself proves. But if we believe that the Holy Spirit guides the church "into all the truth" (Jn. 16:13), then when all Christians can come to an agreement, reach a unanimous consensus of opinion on any given issue, the Orthodox accept this harmony as a sign of the inspiration of the Holy Spirit, as the apostles themselves did at their council in Jerusalem (cf. Acts 15:28). Any individual is limited and can be mistaken. But the church is the "pillar and bulwark of the truth" (1 Tim. 3:15), and the Orthodox believe that when the whole church, clergy and laity, concurs, this unity is given and inspired by God. Most often this agreement in faith became apparent at worldwide gatherings known as ecumenical councils, but the church has also expressed unanimous agreement on certain issues without having a large formal gathering. On the other hand, there have been large conferences whose decisions have not been accepted in the long run as having been authentic declarations of the Christian faith. There is no way to be certain ahead of time whether a particular council will be inspired by the Holy Spirit. In the course of time the general assessment of the whole church, the "mind" of the church, will make clear whether or not a certain decision was a genuine reflection of the Christian gospel.

It was on this conciliar basis that all major decisions affecting church life were made. It was by the consensus of the entire church that certain writings were included or excluded from the New Testament. We often accept the Bible as something "self-evident" as if it were given by God "from the sky" or dictated directly to the evangelists by some angel and automatically recognized as divinely inspired by all Christians. This is hardly what happened! The church began fifty days after Christ's resurrection and had only Old Testament Scriptures to read for the next thirty to sixty years. Even when Saint Paul's letters and the Gospels were finally written, they were of course *hand*written and not every local church had a copy of each. Besides these Scriptures, there were other "epistles" and "Gospels" composed by nonbelievers who tried to eliminate certain Christian teachings by forging "biographies" of Christ, even though their authors had never known him. It was the job of the church, guided by the Spirit, to decide which writings were genuine and inspired. God has always dealt with humanity through *living people,* a community of persons, first the "Old" and now the "New" Israel: the Bible is the written record of how he has used his *people* to carry on his plan of salvation. The Old Testament is holy because the Old Israel recognized and accepted it as holy. The New Testament is sacred because the New Israel, the church, has said so. The early church had to decide other questions of doctrine, interpretation, procedure, and worship, and Orthodox today continue to abide by those decisions. The ancient undivided church still exists as a visible community, the New Israel. The Orthodox concern for history and their respect for the writings of ancient Christian fathers and the decrees of ecumenical councils is not due to an extreme, fossilized conservatism, but to an overriding concern for unity in faith, not only among modern believers but in full *consistency* with believers throughout all past generations, because they believe that the Holy Spirit will not contradict himself. What was true about God, humankind, salvation, and the church yesterday will also be true today and forever. Unanimous decisions of the past are considered as binding as Scripture itself, because it was the church that wrote, edited, and "canonized" the New Testament, *not* vice versa. If the church is "wrong" about any doctrine it would mean the Holy Spirit has deserted it, which is impossible, for then the entire Christian faith, including the Bible, is also open to question. The Orthodox accept the New Testament because the church has accepted these writings as divinely inspired. They do not accept the church because the Scriptures say so. This is a basic difference between Orthodox and Roman Catholics, who look to the pope, or Protestants, who regard Scripture as "infallible."

Another difference is in the Orthodox "definition" of salvation, which affects everything the church preaches and celebrates. In the West salvation is viewed as a new relationship with God. Deserving eternal punishment for breaking God's righteous commandments, a Christian escapes damnation by accepting Christ as the Savior, who on the cross suffered in place of humanity. Because innocent Jesus has taken upon himself the blame and paid the price for our lawlessness, he *saves* us *from* hell by his sufferings.

The early Christians saw salvation as much wider than just letting people "off the hook" for their personal transgressions, because sin and its effects are much broader than breaking divine law. Sin is an act of rejection and rebellion, of separation, and human beings were originally intended to be the "link" between God and his creation. Adam's sin affects the whole world. Life is from God, and to reject him means to turn away from life. It means death. Sin is therefore foolish and even suicidal. When Saint Paul writes that the wages of sin is death, he means that death comes quite logically from sin, not because someone broke the rules and God imposed the "death penalty," but because by deliberately cutting oneself off from life, from God, death is the natural consequence. God never desired the death of sinners but, rather, that they should repent (change their direction, their aim) and live. He never wanted anyone to suffer pain, disease, sorrow, sickness, or death. Only the Evil One engineers evil, but by rejecting God people have become subject to Satan because the fear of death leads to all sorts of other evils. In order first to survive and later to live comfortably, humans must compete against each other. Self-preservation, self-interest, and self-glorification become "natural instincts." Because of death, people steal, lie, kill, covet, blaspheme, and commit further sins. So we are caught in a vicious cycle. Sin has brought death, and death causes more sin. Salvation requires first of all the destruction of death, and second, the elimination of sin. When Christ on the cross said, "It is finished," he meant the whole plan that God had put into operation with Abraham was complete. He had offered himself to the Evil One as "bait" and the devil had fallen into the trap. The Light and Life of the world became flesh and accepted even to die. But when light comes into darkness, the darkness is destroyed. When the Life of the world entered death, death was abolished. At the very moment Christ "gave up the ghost," the bodies of the saints arose. It is Christ's voluntary death that saves us, not his agony (which is not emphasized in Orthodox piety). For this reason the Eastern church observes the Pascha (Easter) at midnight, the time when the Bridegroom comes. That night becomes "Bright" as worshipers fill the darkness with their candles singing, "Christ is risen from the dead, by his death he has trampled down death, and given life to those in the tombs." The Scripture lesson for that celebration is the prologue to the Gospel of John (1:1–17). The most important event in Orthodox religious life is the joy and beauty of that glorious night. Death is dead. God, in his humility and love, has triumphed. The faithful greet one another exclaiming, "Christ is risen!" This is the essence of the good news.

In order for Christ's victory to become our own, however, we must be united to him, but in order to be connected to God we must first be made holy. "You must be holy, for I am Holy." We are not only saved *from* punishment but saved *for* eternal, divine life.

The defeat of death will not be final unless we are restored to unity with life. God's plan accomplished this as well, when, in the night he was betrayed, Christ took bread, and broke it and gave it to his disciples saying, "Take, eat, . . . drink of this, all of you." In Eden the world was blessed and given to Adam as a means of constant contact with God—all except one tree. The "forbidden fruit" no matter what else it might mean, is a symbol of food and therefore life *without* God. In the Eucharist, Christ has made food once again "communion" and thus restored food to what it was meant to be all along. The last half of the sixth chapter of

John's Gospel, in which Christ calls himself the "living bread," and the "bread that came down from Heaven" have always been accepted without trying to explain how "this man can give us his flesh to eat." It is a mystery, as life and love are indefinable mysteries. The Orthodox receive the bread and cup because Christ has commanded it, believing that this is God's way of restoring us to contact, cooperation, and communion with him and each other.

The law had no such power to transform life, as Saint Paul writes: "the good I want to do, I do not do, and the evil I do not want to do, I do any way, despite my conscious desire to avoid it . . . there is in me a power that works against the Law of Good. Who will save me from this wretched condition?" (cf. Rom. 7). The answer is, of course, Christ. He comes to strengthen and uplift, to make holy again those who accept his invitation to deny their old selfish, self-centered, self-glorifying habits and, like him, take up their cross and follow him.

The Christian life is struggle, a battle against "principalities, . . . against the world rulers of this present darkness (Eph. 6:12). It requires perseverence and determination in order to reach the goal of "growth to the fullness of the stature of Christ" (cf. Phil. 3:14; Eph. 4:13), and we know that for the human being alone, this task is impossible. With God, in cooperation with him in faith, hope, and love, "all things are possible." The Orthodox honor the saints of past ages because they proved by their lives, in prayer, self-denial, faith, and love, in living in communion with God through his church, that holiness, union with God, God-likeness is possible. The commandment to be "perfect as Our Heavenly Father" is not unfulfillable. We are today "called to be saints" as the Christians of Corinth were (1 Cor. 1:2) but, with the apostle, we must admit that we have not yet reached that perfection (cf. Phil. 3:12).

Salvation *for* eternal life as participating in the "divine nature" (2 Pet. 1:4) begins as a process at baptism, by which we are adopted as children of God, granted citizenship in his kingdom." In the world to come, this process will increase our joy as we draw ever nearer to God without struggle. In this life, however, the growth requires constant effort, and we are promised only tribulation. The Christian life is "spiritual warfare," in which prayer, fasting, and all acts of charity and goodwill for the sake of Christ are the main weapons, and the holy mysteries are the chief sources of strength and power together with the Bible and other spiritual literature. Born into a fallen, deformed world, all of us are defective by being part of a creation separated from God. A person can be a complete human being only by being restored to union with God. A person without God is the unfinished plan of a human being. In the church, "which is his body, fullness of him who fills all in all" (Eph. 1:23), the fullness of life is available once again. All creation is affected by this, since "all things were created through him and for him. He is before all things, and in him all things hold together" (Col. 1:16–17). His work of healing, forgiving, restoring, and sanctifying is being continued by his mystical body, the church. He is "with us always" and through the Holy Spirit he renews the world *now*.

According to the account in Genesis, paradise was filled with God's presence, and in the end Christ will be again "all in all." In the meantime, the world is being prepared for that final transformation as Christ makes "all things new" in history. Creation is being restored, for Christ comes to save not only human souls but the "world" which God so loved. Just as Christ's body did not disintegrate or totally spiritualize after his resurrection, so shall we and all creation be transfigured—not annihilated or abolished in the kingdom. The mission of the church extends to all things as well as to all humanity. Creation must be reclaimed, returned to its proper relation to God, to its proper function as a sign of God's presence and love given to humanity. This sacramental character of creation must be restored as part of the saving commission to preach the gospel "to all creatures," to make "all things new" *now*.

The Orthodox church witnesses to this vision of salvation *for* holiness, *for* all creation in art, music, and architecture, and in a rich liturgical life in which the material world is used in its original and proper function to the glory of God. In the divine liturgy, the Orthodox "communion service," the Orthodox participate in the reality of heaven, in the worship of the saints and angelic choirs, which goes on eternally in the kingdom of God. The entire service is sung (except, of course, for the sermon) and everything is done in the most beautiful way possible, in order to communicate the joy and glory that has become accessible to believers. The church building is designed according to a definite plan, with three sections, including the Holy of Holies, which contains the altar table (more correctly the "throne" on which the Lamb sits), together with the seven candlesticks, the incense, and special vestments, as in the biblical visions of heaven (cf. Exodus 25, Ezekiel 43, Isaiah 6, and especially Revelation 1, 7, 8).

The liturgy is always offered by the local church, the people of God gathered in that place, "on behalf of the whole world," for "all mankind," as the prayers of the Anaphora, or offering, explicitly state. The Christians, by coming together, become something they cannot be alone at home. They become the church. The celebrant comes early to prepare the gifts of bread, wine, and water according to a special rite, first cutting the bread, "in honor and in memory of Our Lord and God and Savior Jesus Christ," and then in memory of the Virgin Mary "Who gave birth to God the Word," the saints and prophets of the Old Testament, early martyrs and apostles, church fathers, ascetics and healers, as well as the living and departed members of the local community, all of whom are mentioned by name. This offering of food, which is necessary to sustain our life, and can thus represent our life, will be brought to the altar during the last part of the service.

The public segment of the liturgy begins with a blessing of the kingdom of the Father, Son, and Holy Spirit, and in this way declares the kingdom to be our goal, in this gathering and in our entire life. The "Liturgy of the Catechumens" has as its theme the coming and the preaching of the Word of God. After singing responsively several psalms and litanies, the celebrants carry the Gospel book in procession to the altar. The choir then joins the heavenly angelic chorus by singing the hymn, "Holy, Holy, Holy," as a liturgical affirmation that we have entered God's presence and he is about to speak to us in the readings from the Scriptures. The first section of the liturgy ends with the sermon, as the first type of communion "in the Spirit" of which the faithful partake.

The next part, the "Liturgy of the Faithful," includes a second procession, this time of the bread, water, and wine to the throne of God, where they are offered, lifted up, "on behalf of everyone and for everything." After invoking the Holy Spirit to descend and transform the humble gifts into the very body and blood of

Christ, the Eucharist is fulfilled as the faithful receive the "Heavenly Bread and the Cup of Life." They then return "to the world" strengthened and sanctified by the holy mysteries, ready to continue their struggle toward God-likeness, asking Christ to "keep them in His Holiness." God is not a distant Lord whom we learn *about* through the study of books alone. He is a living God whom we personally *know,* who teaches, forgives, heals, sanctifies, encourages, and fortifies us, who comes into us as the living bread and abides in us and we in him (cf. John 6). The Orthodox considers defining *how* it is possible to "eat his body and drink his blood" as beyond human reason, but because Christ has said, "Unless you eat the flesh of the Son of Man and drink his blood, you have no *life* in you," the church believes and obeys without demanding explanations.

Orthodox Mission

From what has been said about the Orthodox concept of salvation as a continuing process of growth toward God-likeness through spiritual warfare, we can understand why the church's approach to mission is not restricted to bringing the Christian faith to new geographic areas, but emphasizes intensifying and deepening the understanding and commitment of those who have already become members of the church as well. No matter how far anyone has progressed toward full humanness, each person has *infinitely* more to grow. The church sets no minimums: there is only the *maximum*—holy as God is holy, that is, *Christ*—for our goal. No territory, no individual can be considered permanently, irreversibly "saved." The Evil One is a tireless enemy who will try to subvert even the saints. The battle never ends in this world. Each believer must remember how even in the original Twelve, Satan was able to tempt and recapture Judas. To relax is to invite disaster. "Watch and pray," the Lord advised, "lest you enter into temptation. The spirit is willing but the flesh is weak."

In evangelizing new territories, the Eastern church has often resorted to establishing monastic communities as "outposts" of Christian life, where the gospel could be presented by example as much as by preaching. The personal life of committed Christians living among non-Christians often has a greater influence on the attitudes of the unbelievers than the spoken word. God has always dealt with people by sending his people, not written messages. Authentic holiness attracts those who seek the truth. Remote deserts and forests are redeemed in this way, sanctified, reclaimed by being inhabited, and therefore no longer the domain of the Evil One, since life has entered and occupied them. From an Orthodox point of view, such a mission would be a success even if no human beings were converted, just as the presence of the prophet Elijah, John the Baptist, and Jesus Christ himself in the Judean wilderness "reconquered" that land and transformed it into the Hold Land. Not everyone is capable of accepting the call for a life totally given to physical labor and prayer, but certainly some are called by God for this particular vocation. The Orthodox see great merit even in solitary hermitages, for every place of prayer, no matter how humble, sanctifies a given site, restoring it to its proper status as a holy place. This is true, of course, of every Christian dwelling, every Christian home, each containing its "beautiful corner" where the icons, as visible signs of God's presence and holiness, remind all those who enter of the high calling all Christians share.

There are today numerous Orthodox "holy lands," sanctified by a thousand years of holiness where men and women of prayer "keep watch," offering petitions for the salvation of the whole world on Mount Athos and Meteora, in Greece; Zagorsk, in Russia; Valaamo, Finland; Ochrid, Bulgaria, and the painted monasteries of Moldavia, Romania. Other communities have been founded in the center of large cities, since these too were seen as "spiritual deserts": Studion in Constantinople and Pechersk in Kiev, for example. As places of retreat and pilgrimage to which Orthodox believers of all ages and social classes have traditionally resorted for advice, inspiration, and spiritual refreshment, monasteries have been the oases where Christians drank living water. The *evangelical* importance of monastic witness among Eastern Christians can hardly be exaggerated.

The Orthodox faith was first introduced into North America by a monastic mission from Valaamo, which arrived at Kodiak, Alaska, in September 1797. By most standards, the mission was a failure. After preaching and baptizing several thousand Aleuts and Indians, the monks, who were abused by the Russian frontiersmen (who had come to the New World in search of furs, which they obtained by mistreating the indigenous peoples whom the monks had come to convert), either returned to Russia or were lost at sea or martyred by hostile tribes. Only one, a layman named Herman, remained in solitude near Kodiak for another three decades, but by his pious life of dedicated service to the people there, he witnessed more effectively to Christ than any number of preachers of less sanctity might have. The steadfast commitment of the Aleut people to Orthodoxy can be directly attributed to the holiness of life exemplified by this humble monk. He was officially added to the church's list (canon) of saints as Saint Herman of Alaska in August 1970, as a direct result of their veneration of his memory.

The Alaskan mission was further advanced by Saint Innocent (John) Veniamenov, who brought his wife and family to Unalaska in 1824. After learning the local language, he devised an alphabet for it and published the first translations of Holy Scripture in the Aleut tongue. Elected bishop after his wife's death, he erected a cathedral and founded a seminary for the training of indigenous Alaskan clergy at Sitka. He was responsible for the evangelization of Eskimo peoples in Bristol Bay and the Yukon Delta, where he assigned the first native American priests almost a century and a half ago. In these efforts, Veniamenov continued the traditional principles of evangelism established a thousand years earlier by Saints Cyril and Methodius, and used by the Orthodox missions in Central Asia, Siberia, Korea, China, and Japan as well.

It was World War I, however, that brought millions of immigrants and refugees to America from Eastern Europe and the Middle East, who organized Orthodox parishes in the industrial northeast where they found jobs in the mills, mines, and factories. Their children and grandchildren eventually moved to other parts of the country, so that now there are Orthodox churches in every state of the Union. The first congregations brought with them or recruited pastors from the Old World, and were practically "independent," without much connection to any higher church administration. At first the only Orthodox bishop in the United States was in Alaska, appointed by the Orthodox church in Russia, and all Orthodox in the New World acknowledged him as their administrator. The Bolshevik revolution made this situation impossible to maintain, and each ethnic group established its own church administration during the 1920s. This division of the Orthodox congregations into overlapping ethnic dioceses administratively dependent on Old World churches (in direct violation of the territorial principles of church government that had existed everywhere until 1921) constitutes the most serious obstacle to effective Orthodox witness and evangelism in North America. In 1970 the first steps toward a reunited Orthodox church in America were taken, when the Orthodox church in Russia recognized the independence of its former diocese. This new Orthodox church in America, comprised of the former Alaskan mission plus parishes founded by immigrants from Russia, Bulgaria, Romania, and Albania, by American converts and a new Mexican diocese, represents the nucleus around which a unified Orthodox church is being organized. Although the largest Orthodox group in the New World, the Greek Orthodox Archdiocese, is still subject to the Ecumenical Patriarchate in Istanbul, there is full doctrinal and sacramental unity among all canonical jurisdictions in America.

The Russian Civil War did have some positive effect on the church in the United States. Many of the foremost Russian theologians escaped the USSR and founded an Orthodox seminary in Paris, which became a center for the church's intellectual life in the West. This school produced some of the finest modern Orthodox theologians, many of whom have since come to St. Vladimir's Seminary, in Crestwood, New York, making it one of the most important spiritual and academic institutions in the Orthodox world. The dozens of books produced by the seminary press reach thousands of historians, theologians, scholars, and laymen and women throughout the English-speaking world. Original works of Fathers Alexander Schmemann and John Meyendorff are available in every major European language, and have even circulated in the underground (*samizdat*) press within the Soviet Union. In this roundabout way, the Orthodox in America are helping promote an Orthodox religious renaissance in the Old World.

Orthodox monasteries for men and women have been established in Pennsylvania, New York, Massachusetts, Georgia, California, and Mexico. The total Orthodox population in the

United States numbers close to 5 million. As Orthodox immigration decreases, and second- and third-generation American-born church members disperse to other sections of the country, new Orthodox parishes are being organized, particularly in the south. The Orthodox church in America has recently established a new diocese, which includes dozens of communities in Georgia, Mississippi, Alabama, Louisiana, Tennessee, Florida, and Texas, where the bishop, a convert to Orthodoxy, resides. At St. Augustine, Florida, site of an early community of Greek immigrants, a National Greek Orthodox center has been established, the St. Photios Shrine. The dynamic and "progressive" mission in Florida, through the use of Spanish, has attracted many Latin Americans who were searching for spiritual truth. Most of the new parishes are multi-ethnic in national identity, and use English in their liturgical and religious-education programs. The combination of excellent theological literature about Orthodoxy and the existence of an increasing number of active congregations worshiping in English across the nation has attracted hundreds of converts to the Orthodox church in the past decade. Coupled with a liturgical and sacramental renewal in the older parishes of the northeast, these developments herald a new era of growth and stability for the Orthodox church in the United States.

The mission to Orthodoxy in America therefore includes: (1) the preaching and celebration of the Christian faith in its fullness as it was proclaimed and defined by the ancient undivided church; (2) the restoration and sanctification of the created world, through private prayer and public worship, particularly in monastic life; (3) the deepening of the commitment and understanding of the faith by those already baptized into the church (who are waging "spiritual warfare" in their continuing struggle toward full humanness, God-likeness, holiness), through intensive educational programs organized by the theological seminaries; (4) the administrative unification of all "ethnic" jurisdictions into one canonically independent (autocephalous) church in America; (5) the geographic expansion of the church through the founding of multi-ethnic "mission parishes"; (6) active spiritual and material assistance to the Orthodox churches in the Old World and to Orthodox missions in Asia, Africa, Latin America, and Australia—a role already being filled by the creativity and vitality of theological thought being displayed by the faculty of St. Vladimir's. As the Orthodox church strives toward the realization of these goals, the entire population of the United States will benefit, for the church is that "leaven" by which the whole loaf is "enlivened" and transformed. As an ancient tradition whose "identity" was not formed by the Reformation, Orthodox theology offers fresh insights into the message and mission of the Christian faith, which may open new channels for ecumenical dialogue and witness to the modern world.

Melbourne 1980: The Orthodox Dilemma

I

It is from this historical, theological, and spiritual context that an American Orthodox participated in the Melbourne Conference in 1980. The lack of Pan-Orthodox unity on the administrative level hampered the effectiveness of the Orthodox witness throughout the conference, and the almost total lack of daily Orthodox services rendered Orthodox contributions in Section III (The Church Witnesses to the Kingdom) abstract theory rather than immediate experience. In the light of the foregoing introduction to the Orthodox perspective on mission, this lack of concrete liturgical witness (the church being actualized as the "icon of the kingdom" already present in this world) represented a serious deficiency. While Orthodox theologians insisted on the centrality of liturgical and especially eucharistic experience in the Christian life, the divine liturgy was celebrated only once by the Orthodox delegation during the two-week conference. This contrasted with various Western denominations whose tradition does not include the liturgical emphasis of the Christian East, but which nevertheless worshiped daily as a group.

The Orthodox met in Dandenong, south of Melbourne, for one afternoon before the full conference gathered, but the proceedings were limited to the reading of two theological papers and a good deal of socializing. The entire delegation from the USSR arrived too late and too exhausted to attend this business session, and the already existing cultural and political isolation of the Russian, Georgian, and Ukrainian clergy was certainly aggravated by this unfortunate absence.

At the Melbourne Conference, therefore, an American Orthodox served a unique inter-Orthodox function: being the representative of an autocephalous church established by the church of Russia, and also being personally acquainted with participants from Greece, Finland, Romania, Bulgaria, and the local Australian clergy. In the capacity of a liaison, I was able to gather some of the Orthodox representatives for an early liturgy on the Feast of Our Lord's Ascension, celebrated by Metropolitan Antony of Leningrad and me on the University of Melbourne campus. At a luncheon hosted by the American delegation for the twenty participants from the Soviet Union, I, as the only person present with close spiritual and personal ties with both countries, had the honor of proposing a toast to peace and cooperation between the two nations.

It was, however, paradoxically important for the Orthodox church in America to take an emphatic stand on the subject of persecution of believers in the USSR, especially in the wake of the arrest of Father Dmitri Dudko, whose writings had already been translated and published in the United States by my own Alma Mater, St. Vladimir's Seminary. In committee and plenary sessions, and on Australian public radio, I spoke in defense of Father Dudko, Father Yakunin, and others, asking that their plight be explicitly noted by the World Council of Churches in much the same way specific injustices in other countries were decried. These efforts were discouraged by the WCC administration, who refused to allow photocopying of my appeal on behalf of persecuted Christians in the Soviet Union (as potentially "embarrassing" to the Russian delegation), while encouraging Third World delegates to criticize the political, social, and economic oppression in their homelands. This double standard created much dissatisfaction among free Orthodox delegates, but the exceptionally small number of free Orthodox at Melbourne limited the impact of this alienation. Much Orthodox dissatisfaction and ineffectiveness, therefore, can be attributed to the Orthodox themselves. Not only were the conference themes ignored at the preconference meeting in Dandenong, but no coordinated effort at presenting a consistent Orthodox liturgical/theological witness was ever attempted.

II

The deeper frustration experienced by Orthodox participants in ecumenical affairs, however, arises from the theological and spiritual situation outside the Orthodox communion. It is this fundamental anxiety, more than chronic internal inefficiency, that calls into question the very nature of Orthodox involvement in the World Council. A leading American Orthodox theologian has termed this the "agony" of the Orthodox, and Melbourne represented yet another manifestation of this continuing tragedy.

The "pain" that an Orthodox Christian experiences in ecumenical discussion stems from the thousand years of separation from the West, during which the "occidental mind" underwent a tremendous metamorphosis. While continuing to employ identical theological terms and scriptural texts to describe their faith, Eastern and Western Christians began to attach quite different meanings to their common vocabulary. In Melbourne the very word "church" became a subject of such controversy that, as the final session prepared to adjourn, the Orthodox delegations virtually erupted in a belated and unsuccessful attempt to articulate a traditional Orthodox vision of what the church is. The frustration at being misunderstood due to historical and cultural circumstances is further complicated by the Western tendency to categorize everyone and everything as an essential first step in dealing with reality. The East has traditionally opposed defining and classifying reality, believing instead that life, love, faith (and all divine attributes) are essentially irreducible to human language. The Easterner comes with a much less specialized vocabulary and therefore use of a given term is almost always less restricted, less precisely defined than in the Western usage.

Besides this very basic difference, the Orthodox find themselves and their entire tradition classified as "ancient" (or stubbornly conservative), bound by highly dogmatic (or counterproductive) "customs," richly "liturgical," and deeply "spiritual." Since WCC conferences include increasing numbers of laity from all Christian traditions, these prejudices about the Orthodox church are compounded by the general ignorance of its faith and tradition by the vast majority of delegates. What the non-Orthodox does know about the Orthodox church influences him or her to categorize it, and what he or she does not know makes real communication, from a traditional Orthodox perspective, practically impossible. Orthodox delegates spend most of their time attempting to educate others about themselves and their faith as a preliminary step toward genuine discussion, while Protestant participants want to address the issues they see as immediately relevant. The Orthodox find themselves talking about the past, while the Protestant majority is concerned with the latest economic, social, political, and theological "fads." Worship throughout the conference requires that the Orthodox "acculturate" and adopt Protestant forms and attitudes foreign to their whole tradition, producing a sense of oppression for those who participate in ecumenical events in order to witness to this very tradition.

In addition to these sensitive and difficult issues, the theological fragmentation of modern Western Christendom divides the WCC into interest groups or factions, each with its own special issue to present. Each "party" struggles against the others for time to present its main concerns and lobby in favor of them. Each seeks the World Council's blessing for its particular position, tactic, or goal as *the* Christian position, method, or ideal. The conflicts and controversies of modern life invade doctrinal and liturgical discussion on every level. Leftists, feminists, democrats, and revolutionaries struggle to win support for their "party," and the Orthodox are placed in the same category, as just one more (though certainly more exotic) "faction" seeking recognition from the WCC.

The Orthodox self-concept for membership in the World Council is not conceived in this way. The poorly organized and unenthusiastic participation of the Orthodox churches in ecumenical dialogue represents ambivalence toward the World Council arising from this colossal breakdown in cross-cultural interecclesial communication. The Orthodox see their "mission" within the WCC as a challenge to the Protestant tradition to recognize that the Western vision of the Christian faith is itself limited by historical/cultural events, while the West attempts to squeeze the

Orthodox into those very categories that so restrict its perception. The East meets the West in order to indicate that there is much more to the Christian faith we share than either of us suspects— much of it indefinable—and that there is and always has been a balanced and complete theological, spiritual, and dogmatic vision that alone constitutes the *context* in which all the particular issues confronting Western secular society can be addressed. The Orthodox see no real hope in resolving the conflicts of male/ female, rich/poor, capitalist/communist/anarchist outside this catholic (balanced and complete) worldview. This is precisely what the Orthodox "lobby" is. The frustration of being relegated to the status of just one more "interest group" within the WCC leads the Orthodox to adopt a rather pessimistic attitude toward the future of the ecumenical movement. How the World Council of Churches needs to be restructured in order to allow the Orthodox to participate with more enthusiasm (or at least less frustration) and how the Orthodox churches need to reassess their involvement and articulate their faith in terms comprehensible to Western Protestant laity require careful thought and prayerful attention in the years ahead.

The final legacy of Melbourne, then, remains unclear. If the experience of being misrepresented and misunderstood due to their own lack of coordinated witness leads to genuine concern and reflection among the Orthodox and ultimately to a renewed sense of unity within the Orthodox communion, the first half of the dilemma will be resolved. But this transformation is unlikely to occur so long as the Orthodox participate in the World Council of Churches as second-class members, forced by the Protestant "majority" to conform to Western liturgical practices and adopt Western theological terminology. Such reevaluation probably will not come until *both* sides are equally frustrated with the status quo, and it did not seem that this had yet occurred in Melbourne. One hopes that with each successive conference there will be a growing awareness that we are not, after so many decades, really communicating with each other—and once having realized this, Christians East and West might be able to sit down and discuss the issues that divide. Then, under the guidance of the Holy Spirit, we will be finally on the road toward that unity we know our Lord himself demands. "Thy kingdom come!"

After Melbourne, What?

EUGENE L. STOCKWELL

We in the United States are not very good at following up world ecumenical conferences. Vaguely some of us know they occurred, but even if they have seemed important at the time they quickly fade in memory. We go on to the next pressing concern, the next front-page issue that seems to demand our attention.

The 1980 Melbourne Assembly of the Commission on World Mission and Evangelism of the World Council of Churches, on the theme "Your Kingdom Come," raised many important issues, as this volume evidences. What is critical for the churches of the United States is not so much that we engage in a systematic follow-up of a particular assembly, but rather, that we give serious attention to the major assembly issues that in our context and daily life can be illuminated and addressed positively. We too, in our country, are called to take the coming of the kingdom as a reality that impacts our nation, the United States, and all of us who live within it.

Recently Bishop Lesslie Newbigin, until his retirement a bishop of the Church of South India and now actively retired in Great Britain, visited the United States. At an informal luncheon with a group of old friends and admirers he was asked to say a few words of reflection on his long and rich ministry. He summed up his concerns in two points. The first was that the greatest challenge to Christianity today is the "conversion of the pagan West." The second was a comment that the evangelistic programs we fashion are usually of little value, but instead we should "follow the out-pourings of the Holy Spirit" in a faithfulness that is forever available and ready to be used by God.

As we look to the years immediately ahead of us in the United States, Bishop Newbigin's insights are of pressing importance, and they respond well to the Melbourne emphases.

I proposed to take these two Newbigin reflections and relate them to the four Melbourne Assembly section reports, tying the "conversion of the pagan West" to the reports of Sections I and II, and the faithfulness theme to Sections III and IV. Throughout I want to keep my focus on the United States and the ways in which we might more effectively pray and live the words our Lord taught us, "Your kingdom come."

There is never an inappropriate time to consider what God calls us to be in the midst of our contemporary history and context, but there are moments of particular change and opportunity in the lives of nations when such consideration is vital. These words are written in the early stages of a new experience in our national life—focused on the extensive changes rapidly developing in the United States under the administration of President Ronald Reagan. It is a time when the "religious right" is riding high, when political conservatism is much in vogue, when "supply-side economics" and "budget cutting" are the order of the day, when military power is enhanced by added billions for armaments, when the poor sense an immense threat to programs that have helped them greatly, and when (whatever one's views about it) a virtual revolution is underway in national policy in the use of our resources and in the role we intend to play on the international scene. Many in our nation welcome this revolution, though none of us yet knows what the full extent and impact of it will be, on us or on others. Many are very fearful of what appears to them to be a wholesale assault on the poor, the minorities, the women, the environment, and even on some of the most hallowed traditional values of human rights and justice embedded in our Constitution. Whatever one's views, this is a moment for reflection and for consideration of new commitment to what God's kingdom is all about, and as United States citizens we do well to listen with care to the insights of a widely representative Christian assembly such as that which gathered at Melbourne.

"The Conversion of the Pagan West"

Central to the Melbourne understandings were "Good News to the Poor" (Section I) and "The Kingdom of God and Human Struggles" (Section II). For a renewal of Christianity in the

United States, biblically based, it is difficult to think of a more important task for the Christian community than to reflect profoundly on what good news we have to share with those who within the wide human family are usually the last, the lost, and the least: the poor who are the exploited, the ones who struggle just to survive, those who suffer inordinate cold in winter, excruciating pain due to inadequate health care, indignity due to insufficient education, those who see little or no hope ahead, those whose life all too often is bounded by crime, drugs, and prisons of concrete and of social exclusion. Melbourne's message is that it is precisely these poor whom God loves in a preferential way—not to the exclusion of love for all humanity, even the rich—so that to align oneself, individually or as a community, with God's purposes means to undertake certain commitments that are consonant with God's own movement toward the poor and with the poor.

We in the West, and especially in the United States, live in a society in which wealth is extolled, almost worshiped. Excellence and ability are rewarded with high incomes. We surround ourselves with the best houses and furnishings we can afford. We are consumers of wealth in quantities unimagined in most of the world. We waste much energy and wealth. We judge success and "what a person is worth" by the size of bank accounts. We amass wealth in immense corporations whose assets far surpass the gross national income of many nations on earth. We create wealth, we tax wealth, we conspicuously flaunt wealth. We make an idol of wealth—it is the focus of our paganism. Correspondingly, we look down on the poor. We easily assume that the poor are lazy, lacking in merit, not deserving of much but welfare, food stamps, cheap housing, inadequate public clinics.

The gospel judges such a fetish of wealth as sin, pure and simple. The love of wealth is under constant biblical attack throughout the Scriptures. Typically the Bible speaks of the wealthy in terms of judgment and of the poor in terms of compassion. So, painful as it may be to those of us who in the United States are part of this sin—and there is no mistaking the fact that our "Christian" society is riddled with sin—we have to recognize that we are under God's judgment in a most severe way. We may be compassionate of the poor, we may give to charity, we may see ourselves as the most generous people on earth (a pretension belied by the fact that of the seventeen leading industrial nations of the world, we are sixteenth in the percentage of gross national product given by our government to economic development in the rest of the world), but the fact is that our wealth, and the power it provides us, is central to our life. In reality, more often than we choose to admit, it displaces God to the periphery of our life. Wealth is our god, and that is sin.

Is there some way to turn this around, to repent? It does little good to castigate ourselves endlessly for our sin if there is no turning. The Christian community—the church, in its myriad forms—is the place where the turning must begin. We are those who claim to be converted individuals, born anew in the Spirit of our Lord, and the organized Christian community, of which we are a part, is to share God's good news for the poor; indeed, we are to be good news for the poor. But we know that usually we are just the opposite: we are bad news for the poor when we avoid them, when we shut our ears to their cries of despair, when we give them a token of our wealth and no more, when we protect the structures of injustice that perpetuate them in their bondage of poverty.

The Melbourne assembly suggests that churches do four things in order for churches to be good news to the poor, and thereby credibly to be able to share the good news of Jesus Christ with the poor.

First, "become churches in solidarity with the poor." This calls for a sensitive listening stance, first and foremost. It may mean walking to a welfare office to talk with some of the poor in our neighborhoods. It may mean attending a congregation of whatever denomination where the poor are clearly in the majority, to sense their struggles and cares. It may mean reading a book such as Ernesto Cardenal's *The Gospel in Solentiname*[1] to see how some of the desperately poor of Nicaragua throw light on the Scriptures out of their poverty and vision. It may mean taking a youth group to the local food-stamp office and going through the exercises of filling out an application for food stamps to sense what the poor do constantly.

But solidarity with the poor, which starts with listening, means much more. It must surely mean some kind of commitment of life and substance with the struggles of the poor. For some it will start with a public stance against the sin of militarism and the piling up of arms that rob our nation of massive resources that could help the poor. For some it will mean a new attempt to understand the almost unbelievable poverty and exploitation in some other nation—perhaps El Salvador or Guatemala—and a commitment to support new policies in our nation that truly respond to the cry of the poor in those lands. Among other things this may mean not using those nations as the arenas for big-power stages for confrontation regardless of the needs of the people there. For some it will mean a rethinking of our capitalist presuppositions in order to understand that the struggles of the poor are not simply Marxist, socialist, or communist, but a cry for justice devoid of some particular ideology. For some it will mean a personal boycott of products of companies that do a flourishing business with governments that oppress the poor, or that directly exploit the ignorance of the poor. Surely, for all it must mean a biblical search into what God in Scripture is saying to us about the poor, in order to understand why those who engage in that search come out saying that God has "a preferential option for the poor" or that God "is on the side of the poor."

Second, "join the struggle against the powers of exploitation and impoverishment." The powers and principalities are many, often including the church itself, and they are arrayed against those who have little or no power, characteristically the poor. In our power we ring the earth with military bases in order to assure our "national security," but there is increasing evidence we are not growing in either security or respect. Products banned from sale in the United States by our own government are massively exported overseas for handsome profits. Powerful churches and church agencies support counterpart churches and agencies abroad in patterns of prolonged dependency, frequently undergirding elites that are as impervious to the poor of their lands as we are to ours. To know that all too often when we meet the enemy "he is us" is to force us, if we are to be good news to the poor, to challenge openly and directly the powers that mold and control our lives and that at home and abroad reinforce patterns of injustice and exploitation. For some this may mean the difficult and extreme tactic of civil disobedience or tax refusal, in the name of conscience. For others it will mean persistent questioning of our government representatives about policies that favor the rich. For others it will mean checking with the mission agencies of their denomination to see if in fact program priorities aim at the change of unjust structures that militate against the poor. For others it will mean a walk on a picket line against a powerful employer whose actions support injustice. For some it will mean research and analysis into the reality of today's powers—such as the vast influence and control oil companies have acquired, or how private grain companies dominate the flow of life-giving food in international trade.

Third, "establish a new relationship with the poor inside the churches." This is more difficult, especially since in the United States we do not know in many of our churches who the poor in our midst might be, if indeed they exist. Our patterns of residential exclusivist neighborhoods, and churches to match, insulate the well-to-do from the poor at the congregational level. Large denominations, to be sure, have many poor in their membership, but more often than not they are in ghettos of their own. So how to establish a new relationship with the poor inside the churches? It may be important to look again even at our wealthy, suburban churches. Often scattered through such congregations there are elderly poor, too proud to admit their poverty, or the single parents stretched to the breaking point with financial obligations of heavy import, or drop-out youngsters who yearn for a chance at life but do not know where to turn. A recent study of poverty in Lancaster County, Pennsylvania, shocked residents of that affluent farm county by revealing unsuspected numbers of persons below the poverty level, some of them silent members of churches. To identify these poor, to offer them more than sympathy and compassion, and to welcome their participation in the church life, in decision-making, and in warmth of fellowship is a challenge that many congregations have barely touched.

Fourth, "pray and work for the kingdom of God." This, we say, we surely do already. Perhaps, but the focus of this word to us is that churches must not emphasize their own life but, rather, the life of the kingdom and the mission beyond the church, which at its best provides hope for the poor and all humanity. As Melbourne said, "To pray for the kingdom will enable the churches to work more earnestly for its development, to look more eagerly for its signs in human history and to await more patiently its final consummation."

As the church centers down on good news to the poor it will inevitably be obliged to get involved in the human struggles of the poor, and in so doing it will find itself in the thick of its evangelistic task. As Emilio Castro of the World Council of Churches has put it: "The concern for the struggles of the world is not simply a concern for the social-ethical dimensions of the Gospel, but a clear invitation to announce the name of Jesus Christ in relation to the cutting issues of human concern."[2] It is strange, and sad, that we in the affluent West have usually failed, despite all our talk about evangelism and mission, to see that the conversion of the world, and our own conversion from the contemporary paganism we live in, is frequently tied to the poor in our world and in our midst. An example of this relationship is the well-known Roman Catholic priest, the Rev. Henri J. M. Nouwen, author of *The Wounded Healer.* Dutch by birth, but a resident of the United States for seventeen years, and a professor at Yale University, he decided in early 1981 to leave his teaching position in midyear to go to Peru, "to learn from being with" the poor. It is almost an echo of the decision of Dr. Albert Schweitzer years ago to leave Europe to serve the poor and sick of Africa. Neither set out to convert the poor to Christ, but by their lives they open up evidence of God's good news to the poor, and thereby communicate something of the depth of the gospel. Even more than that, they join the poor to learn from them and be evangelized by them, for through them God speaks and evangelizes the rest of us if we are but willing to listen.

"Follow the Outpourings of the Holy Spirit"

Bishop Newbigin challenges the assumption that God's work on earth will be accomplished by the plans and programs we develop, at national or local levels, to bring in the kingdom. Strategies, targets, goals and objectives, five-year plans, and all the rest sound more like a business corporation's assault on a new market than they resonate with the New Testament, where faithfulness and obedience come first and foremost. The Spirit moves in unpredictable ways, and most often uses the available person or community that is readily responsive to the Spirit's leading.

In his own recent life Bishop Newbigin, in retirement, experienced a bit of this. Though retired, he was asked unexpectedly to preside at a meeting of his church in Britain where pastors were being assigned to congregations. Soon it became apparent to him that assignments were made to suburban congregations, but not to the inner-city parishes, and particularly not to one most difficult congregation in a decadent slum of Birmingham. As presiding officer of the meeting he pointed this out, arguing it was less than Christian to ignore the point of greatest poverty and need. The result: open to the Spirit he suddenly found he himself should volunteer for that appointment, and today this bishop of worldwide recognition and influence spends much of his time trying to identify in simple yet faithful ministry with that near-disastrous inner-city congregation. Genuine faithfulness has little predictability to it, but always is vulnerable and available to the Spirit.

Melbourne's Sections III and IV are largely expressions of the meaning of faithfulness in our time. Section III focuses on "The Church Witnesses to the Kingdom" and Section IV analyzes "Christ—Crucified and Risen—Challenges Human Power."

Witness is understood in terms of faithful proclamation of the Word of God, of faithful community living at the local level, of faithful participation in a healing community, of common witness in community, and particularly in the faithful observance of the sacrament of the Eucharist and its implications for the entire Christian family. Interestingly the Melbourne assembly sums these concerns up in what all this may mean "for the congregation where I shall worship next Sunday," and to such congregations it directs five questions:

a. Do we know Jesus Christ in such a way that we can speak convincingly of him?
b. Is our congregation reaching out and truly welcoming all those in need, and all those who seek?
c. Are we expressing the Spirit's ministry of healing for those with broken hearts, disturbed minds, and sick bodies?

d. Are we sharing with **all** Christians the deep concern in our neighbourhood and nation for better ways of living?

e. As we receive the Eucharist, God's all for us, are we giving our all to him and his needy children?

These are trenchant and pressing questions for us in the United States. Our pride prompts us too quickly to justify ourselves and imagine we really are doing a pretty good job on all counts. Think again. At least at Melbourne the very first words of Section IV are "We stand accused." Our faithful intentions are negated and tarnished by our complicity with colonial and economic powers, consumerism, the wasting of persons and communities, shameful injustice in our midst, and not least by our pursuit of wealth and power. But the Crucified Christ challenges human power. Our nation arms to the teeth as our Lord reveals a wholly different power on the cross. Our churches seek for numerical growth while the Bible speaks of a remnant that is faithful. We pore over budgets that always seem to us too small while our Lord lives out a selfless giving that seeks not its own. All this is a hard, almost uncompromising, word for us in the United States. Are we able to absorb it, or at least nondefensively wrestle with its meaning?

It is striking that at Melbourne the Eucharist, Holy Communion, emerged as centrally as it did. That is not what one would necessarily have expected from an activist group of Christians acutely aware of society's injustices. But it did, in part due to the excellent influence of the Orthodox churches.

Listen again to Emilio Castro, as he reflects on Melbourne:

> The Eucharist is described as the pilgrim bread, missionary bread, food for a people on the march. At the center of Church life is the Eucharist, the public declaration of thanksgiving for God's gift in Christ, and the participation of the disciples in the very life of Christ. It is a foretaste of the kingdom which proclaims the Lord's death until he comes. From that center of the eucharistic life of the Church, the proclamation comes naturally, the unashamed announcing of the acts of God in Jesus Christ, the calling to build up a church community, a fellowship.[3]

In summary, if we in the United States are to take seriously the prayer of our Lord, "Your kingdom come," we shall look at ourselves and our nation, first and foremost, as a crucial part of the world that needs conversion, and we shall also commit ourselves to the utmost faithfulness—availability to the touch of the Spirit—in order that God may use us for his purposes on earth, including our land. Mission demands nothing less—and probably not much more.

NOTES

1. Maryknoll, N.Y.: Orbis Books, 1976.

2. Emilio Castro, in *Your Kingdom Come—Mission Perspectives. Report on World Conference on Mission and Evangelism,* 1980 (Geneva: CWME/WCC, 1980), p. 231.

3. Ibid., p. 232.

Appendix:
Melbourne Conference Section Reports

SECTION I:
GOOD NEWS TO THE POOR

The Poor and the Rich and the Coming of the Kingdom

1. The kingdom of God which was inaugurated in Jesus Christ brings justice, love, peace and joy, and freedom from the grasp of principalities and powers, those demonic forces which place human lives and institutions in bondage and infiltrate their very textures. God's judgement is revealed as an overturning of the values and structures of this world. In the perspective of the kingdom, God has a preference for the poor.

Jesus announced at the beginning of his ministry, drawing upon the Word given to the prophet Isaiah, "The Spirit of the Lord is upon me, because he has anointed me to preach good news to the poor. . ."(Luke 4:18). This announcement was not new; God had shown his preference for the poor throughout the history of Israel. When Israel was a slave in Egypt, God sent Moses to lead the people out to the land which he had promised, where they established a society according to God's revelation given through Moses, a society in which all were to share equally. After they had come into the land, God required them to remember that they had once been slaves. Therefore, they should care for the widow, the fatherless, the sojourner within their gates, their debtors, their children, their servants and even their animals (Deut. 5:13–15, 15:1–18). Time and again the prophets had to remind Israel of the need to stand for the poor and oppressed and to work for God's justice.

God identified with the poor and oppressed by sending his Son Jesus to live and serve as a Galilean speaking directly to the common people; promising to bless those who met the needs of the hungry, the thirsty, the stranger, the naked, the sick and the prisoner; and finally meeting death on a cross as a political offender. The good news handed on to the Church is that God's grace was in Jesus Christ, who "though he was rich, yet for your sake he became poor, so that by his poverty you might become rich" (II Cor. 8:9).

2. Poverty in the Scriptures is affliction, deprivation and oppression. But it can also include abundant joy and overflow in liberality (II Cor. 8:1f.). The Gospel which has been given to the Christian Church must express this continuing concern of God for the poor to whom Jesus has granted the blessing of the kingdom.

Jesus' option for the poor challenges everyone and shows how the kingdom of God is to be received. The poor are "blessed" because of their longing for justice and their hope for liberation. They accept the promise that God has come to their rescue, and so discover in his promise their hopes for liberation and a life of human dignity.

3. The Good News to the rich affirms what Jesus proclaims as the Gospel for the poor, that is, a calling to trust in God and his abundant mercy. This is a call to repentance:

—to renounce the security of wealth and material possessions which is, in fact, idolatry;

—to give up the exploiting power which is the demonic feature of wealth; and

—to turn away from indifference and enmity toward the poor and toward solidarity with the oppressed.

4. The coming of the kingdom as hope for the poor is thus a time of judgment for the rich. In the light of this judgment and this hope, all human beings are shown to be less than human. The very identification of people as either rich or poor is now seen to be a symptom of this dehumanization. The poor who are sinned against are rendered less human by being deprived. The rich are rendered less human by the sinful act of depriving others.

The judgement of God thus comes as a verdict in favour of the poor. This verdict enables the poor to struggle to overthrow the powers that blind them, which then releases the rich from the necessity to dominate. Once this has happened, it is possible for both the humbled rich and the poor to become human, capable of response to the challenge of the kingdom.

To the poor this challenge means a profound assurance that God is with them and for them. To the rich it means a profound repentance and renunciation. To all who yearn for justice and forgiveness Jesus Christ offers discipleship and the demand of service. But he offers this in the assurance of victory and in sharing the power of his risen life. As the kingdom in its fulness is solely the gift of God himself, any human achievement in history can only be approximate and relative to the ultimate goal—that promised new heaven and new earth in which justice abides. Yet that kingdom is the inspiration and constant challenge in all our struggles.

Who Are the Poor Today?

5. Poverty is an obvious fact in the world today. The majority of the nations are poor by comparison with the few countries that hoard the wealth and resources of the whole earth. And even within the rich nations there are large segments of the population that are poor by comparison with their fellow citizens. Yet we have had great difficulty in arriving at a common understanding of who the people are who should be identified as "the poor" today.

Part of our difficulty comes from the fact that, although we live on the same globe, we come from different situations and speak of different realities which, although clearly related to one another, have quite different characteristics (context). Part of our difficulty comes from the fact that, although we serve a common Lord and share a common faith, we read the Scriptures in different ways and emphasize different aspects of our understanding of the kingdom of God (content). We have struggled long with this question and hope that further prayer and study and engagement in mission will bring us closer together.

6. We have been helped by a simple definition given to us in one of the papers: "To be poor is to have not, to experience lack and deficiency. . . the poor are the 'little ones' (Matt. 11:25), the insignificant people of no consequence. They are powerless, voiceless and at the mercy of the powerful. . . . The dynamics of being poor are such that the oppressed poor finally accept the

inhumanity and humiliation of their situation; in other words, they accept the status quo as the normal course of life. Thus, to be poor becomes both a state of things and an attitude to life, an outlook, even a worldview" (Canaan Banana, "Good News to the Poor," Melbourne Conf. doc. No. 1.04, p. 3f).

Although at times we have been tempted to contrast "material" poverty and "spiritual" poverty, we have found that an inadequate way to understand the situation. Humanity has been created by God as "living souls," and lack of food and shelter and clothing produces anguish and misery, while lack of identity and love and fulfilment can make even the most affluent circumstances unbearable. The Gospel of the kingdom is addressed to whole people in all of their relationships. God is working for the total liberation of the whole of human life—indeed, for the redemption of the cosmos.

7. We have not agreed on where to place the emphasis, but we have used several ways to identify the poor in the world today:

a) *Poverty in the Necessities of Life*—Those who have been deprived of material and cultural riches. In some situations, this poverty is a result of environmental scarcity, lack of adequate technology and of economies and policies that have been imposed from outside. In most cases, the necessities of life have been expropriated by others in an unjust accumulation of wealth by the few.

b) *Poverty amid Material Wealth*—Those who, possessing material and cultural riches, still do not live in a state of wellbeing. In both capitalist and socialist states among persons who have enough—and more than enough—of the necessities of life, there is malaise, anomie and self-destructive behaviour that has both social and personal causes. Not all of these poor can be described as the result of unjust exploitation. Some would say that these should not be called "poor," although they are in a situation of need.

c) *Voluntary Poverty*—Those who, possessing the possibility of having material riches, are prepared to live a life of frugality or self-denial, in order to make responsible use of those riches. For some this goes as far as solidarity with the poor in which they voluntarily give up their wealth and security to join themselves with the poor in order to struggle against the poverty produced by injustice.

8. We share a common conviction that God intends all humanity to have the necessities of life and to enjoy a personal and a social state of well-being. We feel that this is what our Lord meant when he said: "I came that they may have life, and have it abundantly" (John 10:10) (fullness of life). They are to have life and to share in his life.

Stories of the Poor

9. We have heard from Guatemala of a campesino (peasant) who in a Bible study in his rural village interpreted Isaiah 40:3-5 in this way: The Lord is already near. He comes, but not even the poor are able to recognize him because they are at the bottom of a pit (barrancos = deep canyons), the pit of hunger, exploitation, sickness, poverty and injustice. The wealthy exploiters cannot see him either, because their sight is obstructed by their mountains of money, bank accounts and business.

We have heard from several nations in Africa that some of the African independent churches are churches of the poor that were started because people preferred to worship in a church where they could feel at home as Africans.

10. We have also heard from an ancient church how it has been possible to live for centuries as a church of the poor, being a persecuted and oppressed minority in a hostile environment. This church has sought to maintain the distinctive spirit of Jesus and not to bypass the way of the cross. Its response in the face of violence has been the way of constant love and peace in Christ. The mission of their church, they believe, is to demonstrate the kingdom and to call others to share in its life with the poor.

11. We have heard from Europe and North America many stories of the ways in which a rich society that has provided all or most of its citizens with enough of the necessities of life still has many persons who are needy—where the human condition of loneliness has driven older women and men to alcoholism, where the human condition of lovelessness has caused many to depend on drugs for solace, where the human condition of despair over the direction of society has made young people choose suicide.

12. We have heard from places in Asia as varied as the factories of Hong Kong, the villages of the Philippines, the teeming neighbourhoods of Bombay and the coastal fishing fleets of India, Sri Lanka and Japan how the decision of some of the churches

through the Christian Conference of Asia to be "with the people in their struggles" has resulted in the formation of peoples' organizations that fight concretely for justice and dignity against employers, land owners, government bodies and the far-flung transnational corporations. When the people are organized, they have much to say and their voices can be heard very clearly. In Asia too, revival movements within Islam and Buddhism have reinterpreted their tradition to favour the poor and oppressed.

13. We have heard of the great suffering of innumerable refugees throughout the world. There has been a tremendous increase in refugees in recent years. Many of these are found in refugee camps, where disease and inhuman conditions are rampant. Many others are living in marginalized situations—isolated, lonely, without resources and often without citizenship. Many churches are aware of these persons and join with other groups in various forms of assistance and advocacy.

14. We have heard from Latin America of base Christian communities *(comunidades de base)* which have been organized inside the Roman Catholic Church among the poor, both in the large cities and in the countryside. Led by lay catechists and priests who have determined to live among the poor, these groups are able to study the Bible together, share the Eucharist, develop common actions and strengthen the people of their communities in the struggle against injustice. They have become real churches of the poor. They assume the role of active subject inside the church, revitalizing the spirit of community and of participation, and become the leaven of faith in the wider people's movements.

15. We have been shocked to hear during our time together at this Conference of new assaults against the workers and staff of Urban Industrial Mission in the Republic of Korea—including a large number of women workers—in their continuing struggle for sufficient wages, decent working conditions, freedom to organize and to speak out, and the dignity which God has promised to every human being. In this case those in the church who have chosen to be with the poor in their poverty and in their struggle have found themselves the object of opposition from conservatives in the church and from the government. But the more ruthless the persecution, the more the people who come to join them.

The Churches and the Poor

16. The Church of Jesus Christ is called to preach Good News to the poor, even as its Lord has in his ministry announced the kingdom of God to them. The churches cannot neglect this evangelistic task. Most of the world's people are poor and they wait for a witness to the Gospel that will really be "Good News." The Church of Jesus Christ is commissioned to disciple the nations, so that others may know that the kingdom of God has already drawn near and that its signs and first fruits can be seen in the world around the churches, as well as in their own life. Mission that is conscious of the kingdom will be concerned for liberation, not oppression: justice, not exploitation; fulness, not deprivation; freedom, not slavery; health, not disease; life, not death. No matter how the poor may be identified, this mission is for them.

17. As we look at the churches in the world today, we find some places where a new era of evangelization is dawning, where the poor are proclaiming the Good News. We find other places where the churches understand the situation of the poor and have begun to witness in ways that are Good News. Some of the stories we have mentioned above show the possibilities for a witness with and on behalf of the poor. The base communities in Latin America are churches of the poor that have been willing to share in their poverty and oppression, so that they can struggle to reach a just society and the end of exploitation. Some local churches and church organizations have been willing to redistribute their wealth for the benefit of the self-development of the poor. Some church leaders and denominational groups have been working to challenge the transnational corporations at their business meetings and in their board rooms. Through ecumenical bodies, churches have joined in the search for a new social, political and economic order, and committed themselves to support those organizations, churches and national leaders that share this vision.

18. We have heard of more places where the churches are indifferent to the situation of the poor or—far worse—actively allied with those forces which have made them poor, while enjoying the fruits of riches that have been accumulated at the expense of the poor. All over the world in many countries with a capitalist sys-

tem, the churches are part of the establishment, assisting in the maintenance of a status quo that exploits not only nations and nature but the poor of their own country. The churches are alienated from the poor by their middle-class values. Whereas Jesus identified with the poor in his life and ministry, the churches today are full of satisfied, complacent people who are not willing to look at the Lazarus on their doorsteps. In some socialist countries, although a measure of economic equality has been achieved, the churches have yet to recognize their responsibility toward the kinds of poverty that still exist among the people. And in developing countries, where poverty is the inescapable lot of the overwhelming majority of the population, some churches have been content to make ways for a limited number of the poor to join the elite without working to overcome injustice. We have also heard many stories of ways in which the missionary enterprise of the churches, both overseas and in their own countries, has been financed with the fruits of exploitation, conducted in league with oppressive forces, and has failed to join the struggle of the poor and oppressed against injustice. We need to become more aware of these shortcomings and sins, to repent genuinely and find ways to act that will be Good News to the world's poor.

19. The message which the churches proclaim is not only what they preach and write and teach. If they are to preach Good News, their own lifestyle and what they do—or fail to do—will also carry a message. In his earthly ministry, Jesus Christ was consistent in proclaiming Good News by what he said, what he did and what he was. If the churches are to be faithful disciples and living members of the Body of Christ, they too must be consistent in what they say, what they do and what they are.

20. We wish to *recommend* the following to the churches:

a) *Become churches in solidarity with the struggles of the poor.* The poor are already in mission to change their own situation. What is required from the churches is a missionary movement that supports what they have already begun, and that focuses on building, evangelizing, and witnessing communities of the poor that will discover and live out expressions of faith among the masses of the poor and oppressed.

The churches will have to surrender their attitudes of benevolence and charity by which they have condescended to the poor; in many cases this will mean a radical change in the institutional life of the missionary movement. The churches must be ready to listen to the poor, to hear the Gospel from the poor, to learn about the ways in which they have helped to make them poor.

Ways of expressing this solidarity are several, but each must be fitted to the situation of the poor and respect their leadership in the work of evangelization and mission. There is the call to act in support of the struggles of the poor against oppression. This means support across national boundaries and between continents, without neglecting the struggles within their own societies. There is the call to participate in the struggle themselves. To free others of poverty and oppression is also to release the bonds that entangle the churches in the web of international exploitation. There is the call to become churches of the poor. Although not all will accept the call to strip themselves of riches, the voluntary joining in the community of the poor of the earth could be the most telling witness to the Good News.

b) *Join the struggle against the powers of exploitation and impoverishment.* Poverty, injustice and oppression do not voluntarily release their grip on the lives of the poor. Therefore, the struggle against the powers that create and maintain the present situation must be actively entered. These powers include the transnational corporations, governments and the churches themselves and their missionary organizations where they have joined in exploitation and impoverishment. In increasing numbers, those who will claim the rewards that Jesus promised to those who are persecuted or the martyr's crown of victory in today's world are those who join the struggle against these powers at the side of the poor.

c) *Establish a new relationship with the poor inside the churches.* Many of the poor belong to the churches, but only the voices of a few are heard or their influence felt. The New Testament churches were taught not to be respecters of persons but many churches today have built the structures of status, class, sexual and racial division into their fellowship and organization. The churches should be open to the presence and voice of the poor in their own life. The structures of mission and church life still must be changed to patterns of partnership and servanthood. This will require a more unified mission outreach that does not perpetuate the wastefulness and confusion of denominational divisions. The lifestyles of both clergy and lay leaders need to be changed to come closer to the poor. The churches, which now exploit women and youth, will need to create opportunities for them to participate in leadership and decision-making.

d) *Pray and work for the kingdom of God.* When the churches emphasize their own life, their eyes are diverted from the kingdom of God, the heart of our Lord's message and the hope of the poor. To pray for the kingdom is to concentrate the church's attention on that which God is trying to give to his whole creation. To pray for the kingdom will enable the churches to work more earnestly for its development, to look more eagerly for its signs in human history and to await more patiently its final consummation.

SECTION II:
THE KINGDOM OF GOD AND HUMAN STRUGGLES

I. Human Struggles, the Churches and the Kingdom of God

The many struggles in the many places

1. During the course of the CWME conference at Melbourne on the theme "Your kingdom come," we listened to and reflected upon many testimonies on human struggles. We heard voices of people involved in such struggles during workshop sessions, in plenary addresses, prayer intercessions and Bible study groups. We made use of our experiences during the weekend visits to congregations in Australian churches. For the section work on the theme "kingdom of God and human struggles," we had an introductory presentation and panel presentation from five different areas of human struggles—relating to the sub-themes of our section. We listened to action reports from local situations, where people are concerned about finding the points of contact and relation between the kingdom of God and ongoing human struggles.

In certain areas the churches are confident about the immediate future. They feel that they have come to a "kairos," a God-given time, in which they can join the struggles for a dignified and meaningful life for all human beings. In other areas the churches seem to be at a loss as to what their specific witness should be. In still others they feel overwhelmed by powers working in opposition to the kingdom of God. They see attempts at individual and communal self-preservation at the cost of others and the setting of far too limited goals for communities and societies as well as for humankind and the world at large. In all these situations the churches must continue to evangelize themselves in order to become ready instruments for the kingdom of God.

In the ongoing struggles we hear the groans of the whole creation in all its parts as if in the pain of childbirth. And we who have the Spirit as the first of God's gifts groan within ourselves as we wait for God to make us his children and set our whole being free (Rom. 8:22,23).

The ambiguity of the ongoing process of struggles

2. In view of the ambiguity of what is going on in the struggles, the task of the Christian churches, therefore, will be to discern in each place and context the various tools—outside and inside the churches—that God might use for his purposes.

He has used and uses various cultural and historical, as well as religious and ideological means, for the service of his kingdom.

There is a need for the churches to awaken to their prophetic task in the many human struggles—to say "yes" to that which conforms to the kingdom of God as revealed to humankind in the life of Jesus Christ, and say "no" to that which distorts the dignity and the freedom of human beings and all that is alive.

The churches' calling to live in the midst of human struggles

3. There is a temptation for the established leadership in the churches to avoid confrontation with the struggles of this world on the grounds that the kingdom of God is not "of this world." It is true that it is not of this world but it is "at hand" precisely in a confrontation with principalities and powers as has been clearly revealed to the churches in the life of Jesus Christ. It is our conviction that the churches are called to return to and renew the hope they have in Jesus Christ, instead of succumbing to despair and passivity, so as to be able to join forces with all those who hope.

In the churches' participation in the salvation of God in Jesus Christ through the Holy Spirit, in the sacramental realities of the divine Word, prayers and the Eucharist, they are called to remember and present to God the struggles of this world and intercede on behalf of the world.

4. This should lead the churches to be more sharply aware of their real relationship to the ongoing struggles of humankind and to examine their own structural relations and ideological conformity to the principalities and powers of this world. They should be open to self-criticism and willing to enter into a dialogue with people of other convictions, faiths and ideologies about their own involvement in their common situation. The churches can become aware of what precisely is their witness as

those entrusted with the revelation in Jesus Christ, and of where they can, in his name, join forces with other people of good will.

In their witness to the kingdom of God in words and deeds the churches must dare to be present at the bleeding points of humanity and thus near those who suffer evil, even taking the risk of being counted among the wicked. The royal reign of God appears on earth as the kingdom of the crucified Jesus, which places his disciples with him under the cross. Without losing sight of the ultimate hope of the kingdom of God or giving up their critical attitude, the churches must dare to be present in the midst of human struggles for penultimate solutions.

5. The specific task of the churches is to disclose the final revelation of God himself in Jesus Christ, and by the assistance of the Holy Spirit establish such visible signs of the kingdom of God as offer new hope to all who long for a more human world. Among many young people, in particular, there is a search for reconciliation in the world today. As Christ has come not for a part but for the whole of humanity, the churches must be a means of reconciliation in the midst of human struggles; this will make it necessary to take very specific stands in struggles and conflicts.

Above all the churches have the privilege of witnessing to common hope for humankind and for the whole of creation in the life and death, resurrection and ascension of the Son of God, and that the coming of the kingdom of God is linked with the turning of human minds to Christ as Lord of the kingdom.

II. The Human Struggles Facing the Churches Today

6. In the five subsections, the areas we have concentrated on and the way we have dealt with the problems involved vary a great deal. In order not to lose the concreteness of our reflections and suggestions, however, we present each area of concern under its own heading.

A. The kingdom of God and the struggles of people in countries searching for liberation and self-determination

7. We find ourselves as churches and individual Christians involved in and a part of peoples' struggles for liberation and self-

determination in our own countries. This means that we and the churches we belong to must awaken to the role we are playing in these struggles and be ready to look for God's presence in what is happening, even when he surprises us.

The liberating Gospel in the life of the churches

8. It is always necessary for the churches to return to a full understanding of the Gospel as a proclamation of a message to the world and, at the same time, a proclamation of a way of life. The churches are true to their common missionary task of bringing the Gospel to the world when they let that Gospel be a challenge to their own styles of life and the structures by which they appear to the world.

We recognize that some Christians may feel that they cannot identify themselves with their churches or their own local congregations as being signs of the kingdom because the churches or their established leadership are not willing to evangelize themselves. When people feel that they have to identify themselves with groups outside the church in order to be a sign of the kingdom, there is a great need for the churches to rediscover their own spiritual resources and to care for those who have joined forces with other people of good will.

We are aware of the fact that there are Christians who despair about the possibility of evangelizing their local churches to respond to the Gospel they are entrusted with. A proverb from Ghana says: "It is impossible to awaken anybody who pretends to be sleeping!"

9. We believe that the churches have frequently supported the establishment in order to preserve their own traditional identity and so have ceased to be authentic signs of the kingdom of God. In many countries the struggles for liberation and self-determination have taken place outside the churches and even in spite of the churches.

In a changing world a church that does not respond to the changes is an anomaly. A church that lives in a situation of injustice but is not able to discover in the light of the Gospel entrusted to it the injustices within its own fellowship is no longer an authentic sign of the kingdom of God. The churches in many places have to discover anew and more deeply what the Gospel as a message in words and deeds means amidst human struggles, and what the role of a church as a servant to the Gospel in a concrete situation implies.

10. Again in some countries where independence or liberating revolution has been achieved, the churches cannot withdraw from the urgent task of reconstruction that these societies must face. The Christians are called to participate actively in the process of building the new society. Nevertheless, the churches, conscious of the eschatological dimension of the kingdom that they proclaim, should reject the temptation to develop an uncritical relationship to the governments of their countries. A church which becomes part of the establishment in a settled society is an anomaly. Church leaders in particular must be constantly challenged by the warnings of Jesus himself of the temptation to use authority indiscriminately.

The role of the churches in the ongoing search for cultural identity

11. The previous conference of the Commission on World Mission and Evangelism in Bangkok urged the churches to formulate their own responses to God's calling, that is, liturgies, styles of involvement and forms of community which are rooted in their own cultures. Though this would mean a true dialogical involvement in the local struggles for liberation and self-determination, many churches have not dared to enter into this responsibility. Too many churches are still imprisoned by forms and structures inherited from other countries and are thus not free to establish such signs of the kingdom of God as make use of their own cultural contexts.

The Bible as the canon of the churches' proclamation must be read and acted upon by the people in the light of their local struggles. The churches must live with the tensions between the Gospel and their local cultures. There is the risk of syncretism for all churches in relation to their context, but that must not prevent the churches from struggling with the necessity of relating the local cultures to the kingdom of God.

The prophetic stance of Third World churches

12. The Third World churches and nations often have to answer questions about their alignment, whether towards the

West or the East. Such questions are misguided. What must be understood and respected is that the primary option in those countries as they try to witness to the Gospel, is for the poor and the oppressed and not for the political ideology. The position taken by the Roman Catholic Church in Puebla, Mexico, of "preferential option for the poor" is a clear example of this stance.

In Nicaragua the involvement of Christians in the revolution and national reconstruction is motivating the Marxists to reformulate the concept of and relationship to Christians and their faith.

If a church or members of a church should choose to use Marxist or any other ideological instruments to analyze the social, economic and political situation in which they find themselves, it will be necessary to guard against the risk of being subtly instrumentalized by such ideologies so as not to fall into the same trap as many churches have done in relation to the ideology implied by capitalism, and thus lose their fidelity to the Gospel and their credibility.

The World Council of Churches has expressed in various ways its solidarity with the struggles of liberation and has thus become a sign of the kingdom of God to many people. That sign has sustained them in their struggle and because of this the churches did not lose credibility in the minds of those involved in the struggles. This should challenge many churches to a more overt support.

B. The kingdom of God and the struggles for human rights

13. In the prayer our Lord gave to his church we are encouraged to pray in solidarity with all peoples for the coming of God's kingly rule and that God's will be done on earth as it is in heaven. In the light of this we realize that the structures of our societies—be it the religious, the political or the economic—have become hindrances to, or have actively repressed or even prevented the development of women and men into the fulness of life, thereby denying people their God-given right to dignity and growth.

The worldwide church is itself a sign of the kingdom of God because it is the Body of Christ in the world. It is called to be an instrument of the kingdom of God by continuing Christ's mission to the world in a struggle for the growth of all human beings into the fulness of life. This means proclaiming God's judgement upon any authority, power or force, which would openly or by subtle means deny people their full human rights.

Areas within which human rights are violated

a) *Unjust economic structures*

14. The kingdom of God brings in shalom—peace with justice. Any socio-economic system that denies the citizens of a society their basic needs is unjust and in opposition to the kingdom of God. The churches have to exercise the prophetic gift of assessing the effectiveness of the various socio-economic systems in the world and speak in favour of exploratory models of a new international economic order in the light of the thrust of the Gospel. The churches are called upon to take sides with Third World peoples who suffer from repressive systems in order to maintain the standard of living of affluent countries, and with those who are forced into foreign economic patterns.

b) *Voiceless peoples*

15. The churches have a responsibility to analyze in depth various types of inhumanity and injustice and perceive that some peoples' plights are more desperate than others. This means responding not only to the loudest and most noticeable cries for help but to seek out the overwhelmingly oppressed and silenced to become their advocates and nurturers.

Often the most repressive political and economic systems are not even perceived by people who live under them because they are not exposed to other value systems and options for lifestyles. If they become aware, they are not allowed to express their oppression and their plight because there is no free exchange with people outside the system. In some repressive societies the citizens are prevented from exposing and sharing their pain by threats and reprisals directed against not only spokespersons but also against people who can be identified with such spokespersons.

c) *Escalating militarism and doctrines of national security*

16. The arms race and the escalation in nuclear capability, the failure of peace talks and the strong militarism of many national governments threaten world peace and infringe upon human rights (as is clearly shown in the WCC Executive Committee document "Threats to Peace," February 1980). This situation calls the churches to urge all those involved to look upon war preparations and the infringement of human rights in the name of national security as countersigns to the kingdom of God. It is the task of the churches to plead with all governments to ensure, in the name of human dignity, freedom of dissent on conscientious grounds.

We call for a worldwide cessation of the research, testing and production of nuclear weapons. Unilateral first steps should be encouraged by the churches. We also urge the early destruction of nuclear weapons now in existence. We further encourage our churches to support all efforts designed to place an immediate moratorium on the development, use and export of nuclear power until such time as there may exist clear and enforceable international guarantees against the dangerous uses of nuclear power and its wastes. Also urgent is the struggle against the export of and traffic in arms which often foster regional wars.

d) *Gross infringement of the sovereign rights of other nations*

17. During recent years many countries have used their military capability to intervene in the internal affairs of other nations. It has deprived nations of their right to determine their own future and inflicted further suffering on the people. The result is a new critical escalation of world tensions.

As Christian individuals and as churches responsibly working within our societies, we are called to advocate that our governments respect and uphold the freedom of peoples and nations, and avoid the use of military or economic intervention to gain sovereignty over other nations.

e) *Situations where human rights are violated on the false pretensions of ensuring human rights*

18. In many situations the churches as well as the people in general are faced with the false pretensions of ensuring human rights. Christian groups working for human rights, democracy and freedom, have been imprisoned together with some of those they work among on a variety of charges that do not make sense.

A "state of emergency" makes violence and terror the main pillars of the government of many military juntas. Popular movements are wiped out and dissidence silenced. Revelations of mass imprisonments, discoveries of clandestine cemeteries and the fact that certain forms of enforced economic models lead to unemployment, poverty and malnutrition show that the introduction of a "state of emergency" is not meant to protect the poor and the weak.

Similarly, indigenous political opinion has for long been ruthlessly suppressed unless it could be used for furthering the established ideology of separate development. There are countries where the churches together with all other citizens are faced with the fact that the government claims to be pro-Christian and democratic and yet upholds a system by which people are imprisoned or even murdered because they try to organize themselves to solve their common problem. The recent martyrdom of Archbishop Romero and many others symbolizes the role of a suffering servant that some churches may have to take on in this struggle.

Many Freedom of Religion Acts have been passed within our generation on the pretext that such an act will guarantee a religiously plural society, whilst in realty it has been proved to be a major oppressive force for the churches as well as for other religious communities. Sometimes the religious and political freedom is being violated on the pretext that a liberating political system has to be upheld for the good of the people.

Evangelism and mission in the struggle for human rights

19. When the churches and individual members of the churches

get involved in the struggles for human rights they do so because they have seen in Jesus Christ as the Lord of the kingdom of God a radical challenge of all attempts at depriving women and men of their human rights. Churches and Christians are called to participate in such struggles as those who witness in their obedience to the unique character of the Gospel's demand for love towards the enemy, forgiveness, and reconciliation. Evangelism is part of the local mission of the church in the social, economic and political life of human societies. Thus such participation in struggles for human rights is in itself a central element in the total mission of the church to proclaim by word and act the crucified and risen Christ.

In the struggles for the values of the kingdom, the churches must confront the evil aspects of the transnational companies which are, perhaps, the most potent agencies today for the counter-kingdom of Mammon.

The churches, representing the Body of Christ in their contexts, must also structure themselves in a way that allows all to be partners with God and have a voice in decision-making processes.

The churches must speak out prophetically on questions of human rights but must also be prepared to be a people under the cross in their milieu, bearing silent and suffering witness to the hope which is in them.

In the churches it is not individuals who are struggling but Christ working through them and it is through the small events of our daily lives that the wider changes in society may come about in the direction of the kingdom of God.

The churches have to point out these small events in the struggles for human rights as signs of the kingdom and offer them as a hope for the world.

C. *The kingdom of God in contexts of strong revival of institutional religions*

The multifaceted picture of religious struggles

20. In the many human struggles today not least important is the struggle we face in the revival of religions, whether Hinduism, Buddhism, Islam or others. The question of religion touches the deepest points of human self-awareness as well as all the realities

of daily life in the struggles of human beings for fulfilment. As general features of the present revival of religion we notice the urge for a reassertion of traditional values, the search for self-identity, the efforts to find a way out of the complexities of our modern time and not seldom also a new quest for religious experience and a missionary zeal for sharing one's convictions. The character of the struggles in specific situations varies greatly. This is true not only of the different religious communities but also inside one particular religion where there are not only differences between geographical areas, but also within one particular geographical area.

The positive and negative elements of religions and religious revivals

21. The question whether God is at work in the revival of religions cannot be answered by a simple "yes" or "no" response. In the various religions and in their revival there are positive and negative elements and even this ambiguity takes on a different character from situation to situation. Wherever a religion or its revival enhances human dignity, human rights and social justice for all people, and brings in liberation and peace for everybody, there God may be seen to be at work.

Wherever people seek God and even touch and find God, there God is certainly not far from any one of them (Acts 17). The churches should not forget, however, that when these criteria are applied to the history and the present life of the Christian churches themselves, similar ambiguities come to the surface.

A humble and open attitude to people of other faiths

22. The attitude of the churches to the ongoing revivals or reassertions of institutional religions will have to vary according to the specific situation. In some countries the situation of the churches has become extremely difficult, particularly where the revival has led to erosion of civil liberties including, in some cases, the freedom of religion.

The prayer of the worldwide church must be that the Christians in those situations may find strength in the Holy Spirit to witness for the kingdom of God in humility and endurance, that oppression can be met with love and that God may use their sufferings to bring about a renewal of their own Christian faith.

We express our solidarity with them as with all oppressed people.

In all situations of religious conflicts the churches are called upon to help their individual members to re-examine their own basic loyalties and to understand better their neighbours of other faiths. On all accounts, the churches must try to find meeting-points in their contexts for dialogue and co-operation with people of other faiths. The above-mentioned criteria as well as the common cultural heritage and a commitment to national unity and development could be the starting points for a mutual witness in dialogue. This presupposes a mind of openness, respect and truthfulness in the churches and among their members towards neighbours of other faiths but also courage to give an account of the hope we have in Jesus Christ as our Lord.

23. As has been pointed out in the Guidelines on Dialogue, received by the Central Committee of the WCC, Jamaica 1979, a dialogical approach to neighbours of other faiths and convictions is not in contradiction with mission. Our mission to witness to Jesus Christ can never be given up. The proclamation of the Gospel to the whole world remains an urgent obligation for all Christians and it should be carried out in the spirit of our Lord, not in a crusading and aggressive spirit.

"Let us behave wisely towards those outside our number; let us use the opportunity to the full. Let our conversation be always full of grace and never insipid; let us study how best to talk with each person we meet" (Col. 4:5–6).

D. The kingdom of God in the context of countries with centrally planned economies

24. The frequent inconsistency of the churches, the contradictions in their life, their age-old estrangement from the poor, their entente with power—all these factors have undermined the credibility of Christian faith among many of those who are committed to work for a new world.

This makes it urgent for the churches to equip their members to participate in building a better community where women and men live together in equality, justice and the sharing of God's gifts.

The message of the kingdom in the context of countries with a centrally planned economy

25. The signs of the kingdom of God need to be discerned and proclaimed within every society. The prophetic teaching of the Old Testament underscores the conviction that justice, faith and the longing for the kingdom of God are intertwined and condition one another. The eschatological visions of the New Testament and the life and teaching of Jesus himself show that the kingdom of God is not unrelated to the building of a society which seeks equal opportunities for all. In countries with centrally planned economies the preaching of and witnessing to the kingdom should help people to rediscover Jesus as the liberator of human beings from all forces which oppress, alienate and threaten them either in the old or the new structures.

The participation in building up and ameliorating societies with centrally planned economies

26. At the level of practice, faith in and witness to the kingdom of God are not exhausted by participating in the building up and ameliorating of societies with centrally planned economies. Certain lines of Christian action arise not so much from need for political strategies but from the wish to be obedient to the will of God. A truly Christian style of life has to be redefined today, surpassing any identification of Christian faith with any ideological search for moral standards. The primacy of compassion, reconciliation, love of enemy, forgiveness and eschatological vision of history—all these are aspects of Christian faith which are beyond a merely passive participation in building up a new and better society.

A struggle within the struggle

27. To witness to the kingdom of God in the struggles to build a new society is to be involved in a struggle within the struggles, "for we are not contending against flesh and blood." The churches cannot overlook the fact that if the message of the kingdom of God creates faith it also provokes opposition, and they may have to face real problems. They have to be aware of the fact, however, that God, through the coming of some new forms

of society, has opened a new page of God's history for humanity. In the presence of some of these new forms of society, God calls the churches to a new obedience, new praise, new prayer and renewal of their own forms of service to their fellow human beings.

28. The experience of actually living both in societies with free or centrally planned economies, has opened a wide field of possibilities for many Christians as individuals and for the churches, e.g. to speak against the assertion of military might in international relations, to support a comprehensive reordering of economic priorities, to undergird the morality of social structure and inter-personal relations, to challenge the values and consumerism and self-indulgence that could develop in any society. In their own faith in Jesus Christ and in their witnessing to the coming kingdom of God they find a comprehensive and liberating means of interpreting the ongoing struggle in its wholeness and totality.

E. The kingdom of God in the struggles of countries dominated by consumerism and the growth of big cities

The churches as part of consumer societies

29. Capitalistic-oriented society creates constant challenges to the churches in their witness to the kingdom of God. It sets forth false goals for life, exploiting the greed of the people. Christians living in such societies are tempted to acquire more and more wealth and to over-consume. People seldom realize the manipulative forces and powers behind the advertising business.

In such societies there are many, and in some the majority, who are free from the struggle for survival.

They enjoy easy access to all good things as well as to luxuries. These people belong to the inner circle of the system. Others are exploited and deprived of basic needs and resources and thus belong to the outer circle of the system.

Those who are free from material need often find themselves in new forms of enslavement. Quantity of things becomes more important than quality of life and personal gratification replaces concern for others. The search for legitimate security is misused to provoke fear and overproduction of arms to defend the control of the world's resources.

The intensive concentration of economic power attracts people to industrialized centers where many traditional patterns of family and community break down. As the growth of big cities does not provide equal benefits for all, gaps develop between rich and poor.

The Gospel as an invitation to change lifestyles

30. The churches as institutions usually reflect the values of the consumer society to which they belong. The kingdom of God in this situation becomes a challenge to the credibility of the churches. The crucified and risen Christ is a judge of shallow lifestyles and invites the churches to repentance and new life. In many situations today, renewed lifestyles will be the most authentic and unambiguous way to proclaim and live out the Gospel. This will involve forming and supporting groups within the Church which are experimenting with new forms of Christian community and family relationships. It further involves participation in the changing of those structures which cause imbalances in the world today. As those committed to the kingdom of God have become a minority within the secular affluent societies, this task may seem too difficult. Nevertheless, there is a call to those who wait for the kingdom of God to be the leaven in the lump, the salt of the earth and a sign of the kingdom to come.

The witness to the kingdom of God in action for change

31. When Christians convert or change the patterns and structures of life in consumer societies, their witness to the kingdom of God can be taken seriously. This is true also of missionaries who are sent out from consumer societies to developing countries.

The churches are called to conscientize their members about the inter-relationships of the whole world, about the injustice, exploitation and dehumanization caused by the greed for profit and consumption, and provide information and analyses of the effects of the selfishness of the consumer society on its own, but also and even worse, on other societies. A witness in action will mean involvement in the struggles of those in the outer circle: racial, ethnic and religious minorities, women, the handicapped, those asking for political asylum, etc.

The churches will have to promote action and reflection among their members to maximize the use of various gifts for involvement in the affairs of society, including a more accountable control over power concentrations which affect the life of people, such as the transnational corporations.

Special attention should be given to the defence of free and honest information through the mass media which in many countries are increasingly dominated by people who have an interest in distorting the news to consolidate their own power. Christians should be at the forefront of attempts at creating a new economic order and involved in national and international programmes for a more just, sustainable and participatory society. In this context the whole question of ecology is relevant.

The churches should encourage co-operation with groups outside the churches who show signs of the kingdom of God at work on behalf of those who are marginalized by the system of the consumer society.

The churches themselves should take courage to witness to the fact that a general decline in the economy of the consumer societies need not only be a negative thing but can open up new ways of life which better conform to the vision of the kingdom of God.

III. Conclusions

32. The work in Section II on the kingdom of God and human struggles reiterates what the last CWME Conference in Bangkok said, and presses upon ourselves and our churches an even more urgent need to become involved fully in the ongoing human struggles, and become even more aware of the fact that the Gospel about the coming of the kingdom of God is related to the struggles of this world.

We also felt a need to express repentance about our inability to be more specific in particular cases. This reflects both the painful situation many people continue to find themselves in and the sensitivity we feel towards those where specific mention might be dangerous.

The churches have a prophetic task to discern, in these struggles and in the ambiguities which they represent, where the forces of the kingdom are at work and where countersigns of the kingdom are being established. The church must awaken to exercise anew its prophetic role and itself ask for the gift of the Holy Spirit to establish effective signals of the kingdom of God.

There is a need for the churches to change their own attitudes and styles of life and let themselves be renewed by the Gospel which is entrusted to them that they may serve humankind with a true interpretation of what is going on in many struggles, pointing to Jesus Christ as the one in whom God sums up all things.

The churches have a message that gives meaning to the struggles and a message about the possibility of reconciliation in the midst of struggles. They must spell out that message clearly because there are so many who are at a loss and who suffer evil in the many human struggles which are going on in the places where they live.

SECTION III:
THE CHURCH WITNESSES TO THE KINGDOM

1. This title is a frightening claim, but a wonderful reality. It is frightening because it causes every one of us to examine our personal experience of the empirical church, and to confess how often our church life has hidden rather than revealed the sovereignty of God the Father whom Jesus Christ made known. Yet there is reality here. The whole church of God, in every place and time, is a sacrament of the kingdom which came in the person of Jesus Christ and will come in its fulness when he returns in glory.

2. The life and witness of our present churches is very diverse, and it is not our calling to be judges of their value to God. We can only look at some aspects of that life and witness to see how the church can more effectively carry the marks of Christ himself and be a sign of the kingdom.

The proclamation of the word of God is one such witness, distinct and indispensable. The story of God in Christ is the heart of all evangelism, and this story has to be told, for the life of the present church never fully reveals the love and holiness and power of God in Christ. The telling of the story is an inescapable mandate for the whole church; word accompanies deed as the kingdom throws its light ahead of its arrival and men and women seek to live in that light.

The church is called to be a community, a living, sharing fellowship. This sign of the kingdom is evident where our churches are truly open to the poor, the despised, the handicapped, for whom our modern societies have little care. Then a church becomes a witness to the Lord who rejoiced in the company of outcasts.

There is a healing ministry which many of us have too readily neglected and which the Spirit is teaching us anew. It is intimately connected with evangelism, as the commissioning of the disciples by Jesus makes plain (Luke 9:1-6). It has to do with the whole person, body, mind and spirit, and it must be related to the healing gift of modern medical science and the traditional skills found in many parts of the world.

As the whole church is set in a world of cultures and nations, we have to witness to the kingdom by reflecting both the universality of the Gospel and its local expression. As Christians work together to serve the needs of struggling people, so they reveal the unifying power of Christ. As they honour the inheritance of each person (culture, language and ideals) so they witness to the personal care of God.

At the centre of the church's life is the Eucharist, the public declaration of thanksgiving for God's gift in Christ, and the participation of the disciples in the very life of Christ. It is a foretaste of the kingdom which proclaims the Lord's death until he comes. We celebrate the Eucharist during the "in-between," recalling God's act in history (anamnesis), experiencing the presence of the risen Lord, and anticipating the great feast at the end when God is all in all.

3. In all these aspects of the life of the church on earth we are aware of our weakness, our divisions, our lack of wholehearted commitment and our narrow view of what the church is. We have no proprietary rights on the kingdom, no claim for reserved seats at the great banquet. Therefore we seek the mercy and grace of God that we might be open to all those who are in the kingdom, whether or not they are part of the institutional churches. So we pray "your kingdom come," believing that God alone will enable the church as it is on earth to reflect the light and love of his ruling over the whole created universe.

I. Proclamation of the Word of God

4. The proclamation of the Good News is the announcement that the kingdom of God is at hand, a challenge to repent and an invitation to believe. So Jesus, in proclaiming that the kingdom of God is close at hand, calls for repentance and faith in the Gospel (Mark 1:15). The time has come when the ancient hope as expressed by the prophet Isaiah for that kingdom will be fulfilled. Jesus is sent to proclaim Good News to the poor, release to the captives and sight to the blind, to set at liberty those who are oppressed, to proclaim the acceptable year of the Lord (Luke

4:18–19), as Isaiah had seen in his vision. By Jesus, and in his name, the powers of that kingdom bring liberation and wholeness, dignity and life both to those who hunger after justice and to those who struggle with consumerism, greed, selfishness and death.

The kingdom of God is made plain as the Holy Spirit reveals Jesus Christ to us. The Word has become flesh in him, and his followers proclaim in ever new ways and words the glories of their Saviour. Paul says it with singular fulness and intensity: therefore if anyone is in Christ—new creation! The old has passed away; behold, the new has come. All this is from God who, through Christ, has reconciled us to himself and given us the ministry of reconciliation. It is the kingdom that we proclaim until it comes, by telling the story of Jesus Christ, teacher and healer, crucified and risen, truly human and truly divine, Saviour and Lord.

5. There are false proclamations and false gospels, which use the language of the Bible to draw people not toward God as revealed in Jesus but a god made by human imagination. One part of the church's teaching is to help people discern for themselves this distinction.

6. Proclamation is the responsibility of the whole church and of every member, although the Spirit endows some members with special gifts to be evangelists, and a great diversity of witness is found. Both the church and those within it who are gifted as evangelists are themselves part of the message they proclaim. The credibility of the proclamation of the Word of God rests upon the authenticity of the total witness of the church.

Authentic proclamation will be the spontaneous offering of a church (a) which is a truly worshipping community, (b) which is able to welcome outsiders, (c) whose members offer their service in both church and society, and (d) which is ready to move like a pilgrim. Such a church will not defend the privileges of a select group, but rather will affirm the God-given rights of all. It is the Lord who chooses his witnesses, however, particularly those who proclaim the Good News from inside a situation—the poor, the suffering and the oppressed—and strengthens them through the Holy Spirit with the power of the incarnated Word.

7. The proclamation of the Good News is a continual necessity and all people, believers and unbelievers, are challenged to hear

and respond since conversion is never finished. We acknowledge and gladly accept our special obligation to those who have never heard the Good News of the kingdom. New frontiers are continually being discovered. Jesus our Lord is always ahead of us and draws us to follow him, often in unexpected ways. The Christian community is a community on the way, making its proclamation, both to itself and to those beyond its fellowship, even as it shows forth its other marks "on the way." On this pilgrimage, proclamation is always linked to a specific situation and a specific moment in history. It is God's Good News contrasted with the bad news of that specific situation. We therefore affirm present efforts within the church to contextualize the Gospel in every culture.

8. One area of concern is the widespread oppression of women in both church and society, and we look with gratitude and expectation to the work of those women who are seeking to proclaim a Gospel of liberation for both women and men.

9. Proclamation demands communication in deed and word, in teaching, learning and serving. The theory of communication as it applies to individuals and to groups, to listening and to speaking is a considerable area of study and we value the work of those with technical and theological understanding.

We have considered the proclamation of the Gospel through the mass media, and are grateful to have been challenged not only to use the media for the proclamation of the Word, but also to relate the proclamation to the means of mass communication themselves, confronting the powers in the name of Jesus Christ. This will be a part of a theological understanding of communication.

10. Preaching expects conversion. Conversion resulting from the action of the Holy Spirit may be individual, spiritual or emotional—and these three elements are of vital importance—but much more is entailed. It involves a turning *from* and a turning *to*. It always implies a transfer of loyalty and means becoming a citizen of God's kingdom through faith in Jesus Christ. Conversion involves leaving our old security behind (Matt. 16:24) and putting ourselves at risk in a life of faith. This leads to a degree of earthly homelessness (Matt. 8:20), for even the church is only an emergency residence (paroikia).

Conversion implies a new relationship both with God and with others and involves becoming part of a community of believers. It is individual and societal, vertical and horizontal, faith and works (James 2:19–20). It has to do with those things which may not be bad in themselves, but which stand in the way of our relationship with God and our fellows (Gen. 22; Phil. 3:2–8; Luke 18:22; Luke 3:13). It is an ongoing process.

No one can know the kingdom of God present in Jesus and accept that authority except through the Spirit. This is so far-reaching and decisive an experience that Jesus referred to it as "being born all over again" (John 3:3–8) and Paul as "putting on the new self which is created in God's likeness" (Eph. 4:24).

II. In Search of a Living Community at the Local Level, or Living the Future Now

11. The church should be searching for an authentic community in Christ at the local level. This will encompass but be larger than the local church community because the kingdom is wider than the church. The kingdom is seen as an inclusive and open reality, stretching to include people irrespective of their sex, race, age and colour, and it is found in caring and fulfilling relationships and environments where people are reconciled and liberated to become what God wants them to be. It is not self-preserving but self-denying. The kingdom is found in the willingness to accept suffering and sacrifices for others. Also in the willingness to reflect on and respond to needs and ideas beyond our own community, thus entering into dialogue and service. In the kingdom there is love, openness and respect for others. The concerns, convictions, aspirations, and needs of individuals and groups are received with understanding. The kingdom encourages and stimulates the development of the unique identity of individuals and groups within the total human community.

12. As Christians, we recognize the discrepancy between the reality of the kingdom of God and the actual condition of our empirical local congregations. Some of us have therefore sought different ways for bringing the fellowship of the church towards a clearer likeness of the fellowship of the kingdom that Christ proclaimed. The institutional church is not to be rejected as it is one of the forms in which renewal can occur. Under the influence of liturgical and sacramental renewal, charismatic movements and

parish weekend retreats, local congregations are attempting to realize the fulness of Christian fellowship. House churches and other small prayer and study groups are providing greater opportunities for more honest and caring personal relationships than can be achieved in larger groups. Such small groups very often become ecumenical.

A truly vital form of congregational life is known as Base Christian Communities. These communities, arising among the poor and disenfranchised and committed to the struggle for their liberation, express common concerns for identity and a new dignity. They are a gift of God, offering renewal to the church and calling it to a new presence among the poor and disenfranchised.

There are other experiments that arise as alternatives to parish life and that focus on particular aspects of the demands of the kingdom, e.g. seeking a simpler lifestyle, a concern for conservation, or as a political protest. Monastic communities, after a traumatic period of reassessment, are emerging with new confidence in their vocation in the modern world.

Arising from needs within the Christian community, study and research centres, youth movements and various women's organizations attempt to involve their members in the life of the community by focusing on their concerns and challenging the church to recognize them.

Clergy must learn to see themselves not only as the leaders of worship in the congregations but as enablers and coordinators of the various small groups in a district, linking them with each other and with the rest of the church in a united witness.

13. We discover that we must ask ourselves when shall we live in the kingdom, and how do we live the kingdom now. On this we make three observations. First, we are partially living the kingdom. Second, there are severe limitations in our life. Third, we have hopes for our life that have not yet been realized.

The existence of the Church as it is true to its witness is a positive reality. The Church is the Body of Christ, and the witnessing life of the faithful speaks of the reality of the suffering and risen Lord. The whole life of the Church is oriented towards this witness in its total sacramental life—in prayer, proclamation, service and liturgy. This witness takes on different emphases and importance depending on the context in which the Christian community lives. In living this foretaste of the kingdom life, the Church is compelled to confront the values, structures, ideologies and practices of the society of which it is a part.

14. The local community usually includes children. Jesus teaches us how important they are as signs of his love to us. So we expect our churches not only to continue their work of cherishing and teaching, but also to search for the right ways in which children may participate in eucharistic worship and prayer.

15. The Church often hinders its own witness by its actions as well as its words. It is sometimes an exclusive body. It excludes people because of race, sex, class, those who have handicaps and, through its emphasis on verbal expression, those who are receptive mainly through images. It excludes women through its use of sexist language, and by refusing them full participation, especially in leadership. Class exclusion is very evident in the life of white middle-class western churches and those with that style in other countries. People of different classes feel unable to participate and be heard in this church. Racial exclusion may be direct or indirect; in the latter case it often arises in the same manner as class and cultural exclusion. In a similar manner the verbal nature of the Church excludes a great number of persons who find other forms of expression more helpful. These are only a few of the many forms of exclusion that the Church practices, consciously or unconsciously.

16. Because of the victory of Christ, we have hope. We acknowledge our responsibility for the various exclusions practiced consciously or unconsciously. The Church must become a body that is truly open to people. This will occur when the structures and language that exclude persons from its life are removed.

An emphasis on human relationship within the community, which is healing and caring, will speak of the kingdom to which it is a witness. As local communities have courage to examine and challenge themselves as well as the societies in which they live, they begin to realize their witness. Here we see the hopes and aspirations of the people in the surrounding community being taken up in the life of the witness to the kingdom. The Church at the local level also shows witness to the kingdom when its membership reflects the membership of the community of which it is a part.

The Good News, the Gospel of Jesus Christ, remains the witness for which we exist. It is also the measuring rod by which we discover how close we are to the will of God in our attempts to give life to the Gospel in local community.

III. The Healing Community

17. Our Lord healed the sick as a sign that the kingdom of God had come near, and commanded his disciples to do the same (Luke 9:1-6). It is a healing of the whole person—forgiveness for the guilt-laden, health for the diseased, hope for the despairing, restored relations for the alienated—which is the sign of the kingdom's arrival.

Ill-health has many roots: oppressive political and economic systems that abuse human power and produce insecurity, anxiety, fear and despair; war and the displacement of refugees; natural disasters; hunger and malnutrition; marital and family problems; unhelpful attitudes towards the body and sexuality; alienation between the sexes, generations, races, classes and cultures; unemployment; competitiveness; the division of humanity into rich and poor. Basic to many of these factors is personal estrangement from God.

18. The churches in this response must commit themselves in fellowship with those who struggle to rid the world of these root causes. In their healing work they need to give priority to the poor, the aged, the refugees and the chronically ill who are particularly disadvantaged in health care. It is not only that poor countries lack basic medical services. It is also that the medical professions' concentration on spectacular achievement, expensive specialist treatment, and great hospitals diverts attention from basic health care for all.

The churches should therefore:

a) encourage and support community health and preventive medicine, small hospitals in the neediest places and medical care for the poorest people;

b) seek to engage doctors, nurses, patients and patients' families in study to discover how the dignity of each person may be respected, in view of the many ethical questions arising in modern medicine;

    c) establish care systems in the style of the hospice care move-
ment, to balance the care systems to which we have become
accustomed;

    d) encourage Christians to see service to the people as an essen-
tial and joyful part of Christian witness in society;

    e) affirm death as a part of normal human experience in which
the dignity of the person is respected and the hope of resurrection celebrated by the believing community.

19. The local congregation is to be a healing community. The
Holy Spirit uses the loving service and open welcome extended by
the congregation for healing. By listening to one another and
bearing one another's burdens, the despairing receive hope and
the alienated are restored. Those whose wills have been crushed
receive new courage in the caring group. Worship and sacramental life is a powerful force for healing the sick—especially the
prayers of intercession, the proclamation of forgiveness (absolu-
tion), the laying on of hands and anointing with oil (James 5:14)
and participation in the Eucharist.

20. Today a variety of healing methods is practised. The inap-
propriateness or unavailability of western health care has re-
vived interest in oriental medicine and other traditional healing
methods. There are also two specifically Christian healing
developments. The first is the holistic approach—a blend
of psychotherapy, medicine, counselling, physiotherapy, the
Word, prayer and support groups. We commend this form
of holistic care as consistent with Jesus' concern for the whole
person. The second is the renewed interest in charismatic
gifts of healing through which many people throughout
the world have been healed of various physical and pyscho-
somatic illnesses and had their spiritual life quickened. In
some cases, charismatic practices play a major part in holistic
centres. Since scepticism or uncertainty exists among some
Christians about certain healing practices, we encourage
Christians to be more open in dialogue with each other on the
subject, so as to prevent needless divisions, but we also recommend that serious discussion take place about what constitutes
authentic healing. The WCC is asked to provide help in this respect.

IV. Common Witness to God's Kingdom

Common witness and cultural identity

21. In its mission in any culture, the Church is called to witness to the Incarnated Christ, in family life, in common celebrations, in art and in its struggles.

We affirm the need and the possibility for common witness to populations and groups not sufficiently acquainted with the Gospel, both in cultural groupings where the Gospel has never been proclaimed and in societies where many people no longer believe in the Gospel. We must co-operate in realizing where such populations and groupings exist and how they can be reached. What preparations and initiatives to proclaim the kingdom to them can be undertaken together? We must explore how to coordinate the efforts to witness to these various cultural groupings and how to avoid competition and proselytizing. We encourage all those who are working to enable the Gospel to take genuine root within different cultures.

22. We affirm the need and the possibility for common witness to people of other religions and ideologies, especially in societies where these religions and ideologies constitute a majority or have the power of the state at their disposition. Within this framework, we reflect on the role of martyrdom and the special meaning of common witness in situations of active persecution, whether of one church or of all Christian churches. Even churches that are not in full unity must struggle together to join efforts in securing more freedom of witness for all. No religious community, including Christian churches, must ask for privileges which it is not ready to grant to others. Common witness may be a crucial antidote for the attempt to set various Christian communities and denominations against one another in order to isolate them and prevent them from constituting a presence in public life. Dialogue with people of living faiths can show us how they and we may serve the common needs of humanity. We may also discover that God has fresh inspiration for us in the experience of other religions.

23. We affirm that common witness is especially relevant in

pluralistic societies. The churches can best contribute by joint efforts to promote the expression of Christian values in public affairs and in lifestyles. In societies where Christian belief or one church is more closely associated with national identity, common witness provides an opportunity to strengthen the critical function of the Christian faith toward the transformation of the culture. Common witness implies respect for varying cultural heritages and the avoidance of even the more subtle and hidden forms of cultural invasion. The churches use the language of a culture to create genuine and indigenous expressions of faith. The danger lies in an absolute identification with a culture, thus leading to a kingdom of human culture rather than the kingdom of God.

24. We celebrate this common witness of the Church to the world by dancing, singing and eating our food with one another. In celebrating, we witness to the power of the Gospel to set us free. We can only celebrate in honesty if the churches realize the damage done to their common witness by the scandal of their comfortable life in division—we believe that unless the pilgrimage route leads the churches to visible unity, in the one God we preach and worship, the one Christ crucified for us all, the one Holy Spirit who creates us anew, and the one kingdom, the mission entrusted to us in this world will always be rightly questioned.

Common witness in the socio-political context

25. a) Common witness takes place within the context of particular social and political situations, on both global and local levels. The credibility of the churches in large measure depends on the integrity of their moral choices and political goals in society.

b) It is not for the Church to assume the powers of the state; yet the churches corporately and through their members should be involved in common witness and action in the political realm even while recognizing the ambiguities and the diverse views and solutions that may be proposed.

c) Certain social and political situations and options prevent Christians from witnessing together. This may be due to matters of clear and basic principle: in such cases the duty of witnessing leads to a break. If a church member or a church community adopts or condones an ideology of contempt for people in theory or in practice, their stand is an action of contempt for God's love and consequently for the unity of his church, and must publicly be condemned by other Christians. In such cases solidarity can only be expressed by prayer for repentance, by bearing in mind that the oppressors and enemies are, nevertheless, fellow human beings and that there is an element of tragedy, shame and pain in the break in communication and in the sometimes unavoidable recourse to violence.

Common witness and confessional diversity

26. a) We all share in a common basic faith commitment, the core and fount of common witness to the kingdom.

b) Common witness is obscured, hampered or prevented, for example, where:

(i) interchurch aid in human, financial and other forms leads to cultural insensitivity, church dependency and inappropriate lifestyle, which deform the Gospel, deny a culture and bribe a people;

(ii) interchurch aid fosters church divisions, when partner churches, agencies and groups work separately and even competitively in mission and development; and

(iii) interchurch aid disregards existing local churches, their identity and mission within their own contexts.

c) Efforts can be made, are being made and should be made to overcome disruptive efforts on common witness. Such efforts are:

(i) putting together shared resources to be allocated locally in an ecumenical style;

(ii) recognizing national and local councils of churches as places and opportunities to share the strength as well as the weaknesses of all members, not seeking to retain the best assets for each church's purposes;

(iii)   promoting corporate Bible translation and distribution;

(iv)   developing theological training of clergy and laity ecumenically, whenever, wherever and to whatever extent possible;

(v)   strengthening co-operation in pastoral and diaconal ministries, as a means of practical mutual recognition of common ministry and witness, despite the remaining obstacle in the mutual recognition of ordination and as an appropriate approach to overcoming this obstacle;

(vi)   fostering common pastoral care for mixed marriages, co-operation in the use of mass media, the press and publication, common initiatives in the realm of spiritual life;

(vii)   forming lifestyles of churches and Christians in accordance with the local context and in reference to the least and the last in society; and

(viii) respecting the membership and the worship of other churches, and discouraging a competitive attitude towards one another or proselytizing among other churches.

27. To fulfill common witness in each and all places, three levels are particularly sensitive and are to be focused on:

    a) the local and national level, where the churches should seek and foster unity in and for common witness;

    b) the international level, where the relations between churches should be more thoroughly tested towards a fruitful responsible sharing of resources which enhance, not hamper, common witness. We commend the great possibilities of ecumenical team visits;

    c) the interconfessional level where promising ecumenical dialogue is taking place.

We recognize the emergence of new lines of division which offer new fields for bridge-building and which open new areas where we must develop common witness.

V. The Eucharist as a Witness to the Kingdom of God and an Experience of God's Reign

Word and sacrament

28. As we speak of worship and of our understanding of what is central to it, we are aware of different emphases, but believe there is a growing ecumenical consensus. We value the Faith and Order documents on baptism, Eucharist and ministry which help us to see our increasing unity. We would seek to value the spoken word as having a sacramental quality, for in preaching we ask the Spirit to take our crude words and thoughts and make them effective and loving to touch the hearts of our hearers. We would seek to receive the Eucharist as God's word which speaks freshly each day of sacrifice and victory. We believe that as our churches hold together these two aspects of Christian sharing, we may avoid both the excessive intellectualism of some preaching traditions and the excessive ritualism of some who have focused entirely on the Eucharist.

Unity with Christ in his mission

29. "The sharing of the broken bread and the poured-out wine was the symbol Jesus gave to the disciples to show that they were still included in his own vocation to be the Son of Man" (John V. Taylor). They were eager to share the rights of their hoped-for kingdom. But they could not accept the way of suffering which Jesus knew to be his baptism and his cup. So Jesus went to the cross alone. Yet on the very night of his betrayal, when agony and distress were powerful, he offered this food that the disciples might know their unity with him. We are now in a world where agony multiplies, and where there are no easy roads to peace.

On this betrayal night Jesus still invites us to share bread and wine that we may be one with him in sacrificial love. "The koinonia of the church is nothing less than the most literal partaking in the sufferings and the resurrection of Christ, to make up the balance of what has to be endured in order to open the kingdom for others to enter in" (John V. Taylor). To be incorporated into Christ through the work of the Holy Spirit is the greatest blessing of the kingdom, and the only abiding ground of our missionary activity in the world (II Cor. 1:7; I Peter 4:13; Col. 1:24; Gal. 3:27-28).

Unity with the people of God in the fulfilment of Christ's mission

30. a) Communion with God in Christ and community with God's people are two aspects of the one sacrament. Yet often the worshipper who participates in the Eucharist does so as a lonely individual, although surrounded by other people. The congregation is not automatically a community. It may be a collection of isolated persons, each intent on an interior life and a personal word from the Lord. This is particularly a danger in large congregations. It leads to weakness in our witness, for we may have no sense of corporate action in the world but only of private action. We therefore hope that the churches will regularly examine the nature of their community life.

b) We have noticed that there is very often a distinction or even a division between Christians who are socially active in Christ's name and those who offer themselves in prayer, study and liturgy. Both gracious offerings are enfeebled and distorted by such a separation. Social action may become impatient activism supported only by vague ideals. Worship may become a private indulgence with no active concern for others. We believe that both aspects of discipleship are to be held together in Christian life. Gathering *and* dispersing, receiving *and* giving, praise *and* work, prayer *and* struggle—this is the true rhythm of Christian engagement in the world.

c) We live in a world of divisions, and we have become too easily accustomed to divisions within the church. The fact that the table of the Lord has been divided remains a great scandal. There are many historical sources of this disunity. Yet today it still remains a process of the greatest difficulty to bring all Christians into one fellowship at one table to eat the one bread and drink the one cup. This is a weakness for our missionary witness and its root must surely lie in our disobedience. If Christ invites his people to his feast, how can we fail to celebrate in full communion with all those who love him and are his forever? We plead with our churches to continue the search for that unity which will reveal the Lordship of Christ.

The Eucharist—Pilgrim Bread

31.a) There are times and places where the very act of coming together to celebrate the Eucharist can be a public witness. In certain states Christians may be discouraged from attending such worship or penalized for it. We hear of those who come together at great risk, and whose courage reveals to those around them how precious is this sacrament. In other situations the Eucharist may be an open-air witness so planned that many may see it. Such a joyful celebration as this may offer fresh hope in cynical, secular societies. There is, at the Lord's table, a vision of God which draws the human heart to the Lord.

   b) Yet the experience of the Eucharist is primarily within the fellowship of the church. It gives life to Christians so that they may be formed in the image of Christ and so become effective witnesses to him. The Easter celebration (for example, in Orthodox churches), when candlelight is spread from the celebrant to all, and through all to every home, makes this very vivid.

   c) In order that this process of growth may be encouraged, we seek through the liturgy to help the Eucharist speak to our condition. Each Christian minister and congregation has to seek this understanding, and we can only give some indications:

   Where a people is being harshly oppressed, the Eucharist speaks of the exodus or deliverance from bondage.

   Where Christians are rejected or imprisoned for their faith, the bread and wine become the life of the Lord who was rejected by men but has become "the chief stone of the corner."

   Where the church sees a diminishing membership and its budgets are depressing, the Eucharist declares that there are no limits to God's giving and no end to hope in him.

   Where discrimination by race, sex or class is a danger for

the community, the Eucharist enables people of all sorts to partake of the one food and to be made one people.

Where people are affluent and at ease with life, the Eucharist says, "As Christ shares his life, share what you have with the hungry."

Where a congregation is isolated by politics or war or geography, the Eucharist unites us with all God's people in all places and all ages.

Where a sister or brother is near death, the Eucharist becomes a doorway into the kingdom of our loving Father.

In such ways God feeds his people as they celebrate the mystery of the Eucharist so that they may confess in word and deed that Jesus Christ is Lord, to the glory of God the Father.

Conclusion

32. Having examined these ways of the Church's witness to the kingdom, we are compelled to ask, what does this mean for the congregation where I shall worship next Sunday, bearing in mind the global context of our local Christian obedience.

Each of us has to make a personal interpretation in his or her own context. But as a summary we see each of the five chapters presenting a pressing challenge to every congregation.

    a) Do we know Jesus Christ in such a way that we can speak convincingly of him?

    b) Is our congregation reaching out and truly welcoming all those in need, and all those who seek?

    c) Are we expressing the Spirit's ministry of healing for those with broken hearts, disturbed minds and sick bodies?

    d) Are we sharing with all Christians the deep concern in our neighbourhood and nation for better ways of living?

    e) As we receive the Eucharist, God's all for us, are we giving our all to him and his needy children?

No congregation can ever give entirely adequate answers to these questions. They are always a spur to self-examination, to repentance and to growth. All Christians live in hope, expecting the powers of the Spirit to transform life, and trusting in God's mercy when the Lord comes in judgement and kingly rule.

SECTION IV:
CHRIST—CRUCIFIED AND RISEN—
CHALLENGES HUMAN POWER

I. We Stand Accused

1. We gathered at Melbourne in obedience to the crucified, risen and ascended Christ, and to examine our calling to be witnesses to him in all the world. It has once again been sharply brought home to us that the colonial expansion of the West is perceived by many "Third World" people as a barbarian invasion. Not all the wounds have healed.

The end of the colonial era has not, however, got rid of the fact of domination. One power has been removed and seven others have come in. Large parts of the developing world have become an arena and victims of a struggle between the super-powers, directly or through intermediaries. Some countries have suffered military occupation, political repression and ideological aggression. Others experience an onslaught from transnational companies who, with local elites, have established new centres of power that now encircle the globe. Patterns of technological and bureaucratic development produce benefits that accrue to everybody except the poor.

Since the CWME Bangkok Conference in 1973, conditions have deteriorated sharply.

The Asian experience was described in 1977 in the following terms:

> The dominant reality of Asian suffering is that people are wasted: wasted by hunger, torture, deprivation of rights.
>
> Wasted by economic exploitation, racial and ethnic discrimination, sexual suppression.
>
> Wasted by loneliness, non-relation, non-community.
>
> (Report of the Sixth Assembly of the
> Christian Conference of Asia, June 1977)

2. We in Melbourne have had to face the fact that the churches' complicity with the colonial powers, so frequently condemned in the past, has been carried over and continues to the present day. In the consumer societies now flourishing in the rich centres in many lands, good Christian people and others are now, with "cruel innocence," eating up the whole world. A vast fertility cult expects a wild, egotistical, statistical increase, demanding human sacrifice as the price of building and sustaining our industrial cities, in rich and poor countries alike, for the economic benefit of a minority of individuals. The cries of the hungry are lost amongst the pleasures of the rich.

As representatives of the churches of all parts of the world, we stand accused by our own consciences in the presence of the crucified Christ, at our acquiescence in such suffering and our involvement in this shameful and continuing injustice. We accept this indictment not only as representatives of rich churches but also of poor. Just as the rich churches are being asked to share the pain of the oppressed, so the oppressed Christians stand alongside the accused and share that pain. For we remain brothers and sisters in Christ. This is an expression not only of the unity of the church and the solidarity of the people of God, but also of the pain of realization that we are all part of the oppressive world.

We intend that our repentance should lead, by the grace of our forgiving Lord, to amendment, and our intentions are set out in this report. Only as we stand together in this solidarity can we be liberated from being locked into the structures of power in our societies. How are we to understand these powers in the light of our prayer "Your kingdom come"?

II. The Realities of Power

3. The world as created by God is essentially good. The proclamation of God's reign is the announcement of a new order which challenges those powers and structures that have become demonic in a world corrupted by sin against God. The Old Testament traces the long story of the need to ensure that human power is subject to law and to constant scrutiny in the interest of right dealing. Jesus of Nazareth rejected coercive power as a way of changing the world. Rather, as signs of God's inbreaking reign, he had power to

forgive sins, healing power and an authority over demonic, dehumanized powers. He taught and embodied a thorough-going love and a transcendent judgement which presented a radical challenge to the powers in his society. The religious, political and military powers contrived with the power of the Jerusalem crowd to put him to death by crucifixion. The eye of faith discerns in that cross the embodiment of a God who out-suffers, out-loves and out-lives the worst that powers do. In the decisive events which followed the crucifixion, something radically new happened which seems best described as a new creation. An altogether new quality of power appeared to be let loose among humankind. Those who responded, found that they shared in this power. The inexorable bondage of cause and effect appeared to be broken, and they experienced a liberation which enabled them to face their persecutors without fear and to claim that the powers had been overthrown, disarmed, in a decisive way, even though the powers were somehow permitted to function in the meanwhile until the final consummation of history.

The early Christians used many analogies to describe what they had experienced and what they believed had happened. The most striking picture is that of a sacrificed lamb, slaughtered but yet living, sharing the throne, which symbolized the heart of all power and sovereignty, with the living God himself. The principle of self-sacrificing love is thus enthroned at the centre of the reality of the universe.

With this as our faith, what is our response to the shameful realities of our world? How must we confront the powers?

III. Our Response

A. *In relation to powers*

4. The crucified Christ speaks directly to the central issues confronting humankind in both personal and political life. An example may help to explain this assertion. Our generation is earnestly searching for the answer to the question: what does it mean to be human today? How can we affirm our humanity and put an end to all that demeans and degrades humankind? My identity is my tribalism. I exist as part of my group. But my tribalism is not only

the means by which I necessarily express my being, it is also the way—in the form of racism—in which I attempt to humiliate, to destroy your identity, your being. Only if I can, as it were, die to my tribalism ("letting it be taken up on to the cross"), can I affirm my tribal identity ("in Christ") without demeaning you. In this way, the demonic power of racism can be broken both in individuals and in groups, as the crucified Christ confronts the powers.

5. But, of course, not everyone is willing to die to his identity in this way. Racism and other powers such as militarism, aggressive nationalism and super-power ambitions continue to exert a demonic influence with an immense power of evil. How are we to confront them?

So long as the churches use various kinds of power, they should avoid imitating the patterns of the powers they seek to challenge, or else they will become indistinguishable from them. In the light of the reign of God, the fundamental criterion for their use of power must be the good of the poor and their liberation from oppression. With this criterion, the churches may use their institutional power in any way possible, including through the systems of law or in spite of them. The churches will then run the risk of putting their institutional life on the line. In doing this they are in constant danger of being used by the powers. This danger is not avoided by the churches avoiding involvement in the struggle. To stand aside is to be aligned with the oppressor.

Challenging the powers

6. There are many different situations in which the churches are called to challenge the powers. In some situations the powers are clearly oppressive; other situations are "mixed," that is to say that at some points the powers are seen to be acting in ways which affirm the humanity of the people; sometimes by the grace of God they positively embody higher levels of justice because of their responsiveness to the needs and rights of all citizens. The criterion for determining the relation to the powers is the extent to which God's creative, liberating and serving power is evidenced in their actions, and the extent to which equality is established. We have shared experiences from churches that have found that siding with downtrodden or marginalized people and being sensitive to their needs means sharing in their suffering.

7. When the churches challenge the powers in the name of

people who are being dehumanized, the credibility of the churches with the oppressed is put to the test. They lose their credibility if they are not consistent in their concern for the people in greatest need. In such situations the churches act as agents of renewal and they must be prepared to be minorities, but they can be creative minorities if they pick up issues which are vital for the community and thus motivate others to join in the struggle for the full humanity of all the people.

Another possibility for the churches to act as agents for transformation lies in their potential to influence attitudes and values and to raise consciousness. This demands in the individual churches envisioning alternatives in such matters as the handling of violence, the sharing of economic resources, the use of natural resources, the application of appropriate technologies and the different kinds of political organization at local, national and international levels. In particular we believe that a radical change is needed in the lifestyles of those who are not poor.

We have become aware that the powers of the world make themselves felt also in the life of the church. The tensions that are present in the community are also present in the church, and the churches must struggle with these tensions in their own lives as well as outside. This struggle can be spiritually exhausting and we have heard of Christians becoming "burnt out." We acknowledge our need to engage more faithfully in profound wrestling in prayer as essential to our commitment. It becomes therefore a missionary obligation for the churches to develop a dynamic spirituality including renewed resources for education and a supportive community.

We do not, of course, suggest that the church has any monopoly when powers are challenged. God has many ways of working out his purposes of mercy and judgement far beyond the borders of the visible church. His instruments often include the courageous witness of those who do not name his name, the actions of individuals and groups of other faiths and in secular bodies, with whom we can join in common action.

Experiencing the power of the Crucified Christ

8. By his resurrection the crucified Christ has changed the context of human life. We have shared many ways in which Christians have experienced and are experiencing this power of the cru-

cified Christ, foremost in the sacraments of baptism, the Eucharist and the liturgical life of the church. The faithfulness of disciples in "small things" is honoured; but this does not exempt us from responding to the wider vision. The marks of the crucified Christ will determine the style of social action of the church and its members; these are unlikely to reflect "short-cut" methods; these marks are powerfully present in the suffering, imprisonment and martyrdom of Christians today. Those who are persecuted for their faith share too in this experience of their crucified Lord.

9. We rejoice that in certain revolutionary situations of our time the power of forgiveness is seeking to replace the power of vengeance. In other situations the experience of losing status has been the source of spiritual strength. Elsewhere, the churches, trusting in the power of Christ, have enabled ethnic minorities to recover their identity and to stand up against unjust government powers.

None of these situations has been permanently transformed; it therefore remains for all of us to persevere in the challenge of the powers. We cannot, however, overlook the fact that many Christians lack the experience of the power of the crucified Christ. Too easily we are overcome by grief, pain or fear, or a sense of outward oppression. This reminds us that we are never free from the need for renewal and the need to rediscover the strength that comes from challenging the powers.

Suffering and violence

10. We believe that the crucified Christ shares in the agony of the suffering of the world and that the risen Christ can bring about an inward transformation of suffering, so that it takes on a power, derived from the power of the cross. A new solidarity is generated among those who suffer together, and new resources are discovered.

As we think also of those Christians who are suffering because of their Christian faith under different political regimes, we strongly urge that human rights and religious freedom be respected in their case. We recognize with repentance that in the past and still today in other ways, we Christians have not respected religious liberty as an inalienable right of human beings.

11. The challenge of the powers and the suffering which results from it reveals the all-pervasive presence of violence. Violence is a fact of life whatever our situation may be. But it is a fact and not fate, and Christians must therefore resolutely resist the power of violence.

We are aware that Christians today choose different ways to resist violence. We wish to affirm the practice of non-violence as an inalienable part of the Christian obedience, and we call on the churches to provide support for all those who commit themselves to the life of non-violence. In certain cases redemptive and vicarious suffering such as that of our Lord may have to be chosen by his followers to counteract violence by suffering love—the way of the cross. Nevertheless there are situations in which Christians find their communities involved in violence and, in these circumstances, without identifying totally with any political movement, the churches should act out in concrete forms their solidarity with those Christians and others who become involved in counter-violence in order to free themselves from the unbearable violence of the oppressors. It is necessary for all to take into account that the global threat caused by increased militarism may in the years ahead give added importance to the option of non-violence.

The difference just described which separates Christians regarding the morality of violence is not a complementary harmony but an unresolved ecumenical debate, which this conference has not studied directly. The urgency of this debate is increased by political developments of recent years. We urge the WCC to give priority to direct study of this problem.

B. In relation to church structures

12. Our response to dehumanization and oppression cannot be, as it were, from an innocent church to a guilty world, for we know to our shame that power exercised within the church (in the empirical reality of its earthly form) can be abused. Judgement must begin at the household of God.

13. We have to discern how we may judge whether power is for or against God. What are the criteria by which we make that judgement?

a) Fundamentally we have to ask how the power is used. Is it used for self-aggrandisement and self-preservation of the community, institution or leader, or is it essentially selfless?

When we look at a community, for instance, do we see it as being primarily concerned with the needs of those who are poor and have no power—they may be inside or outside the community—or is it preoccupied with its own rights, privileges and future? We have to ask whether it belongs in sympathy and identification with the oppressed or whether it finds its home with the oppressors.

b) Turning to leadership, we must pose two questions. The first concerns motive, and asks whether the power is exercised as an expression of selfless love, which serves to release and encourage the gifts contained within the community on whose behalf the power is exercised for the fulfilment of its true purpose, or whether the leadership draws on these gifts for its own purpose. A church within which power is exercised in humility and love stands as a sign of the kingdom to the world.

c) But motive alone is an inadequate test. Those who use power are prone to self-deception about motives and the effectiveness of their methods. Churches and their leaders must seek the perceptions of the community on whether their power is helping to free the poor and oppressed. The exercise of leadership has an edifying purpose: it is to build up the body so that every member may attain to the fulness of the maturity of the stature of Christ, in order that they may realize their full humanity. This, it must be noted, does not imply the development of a new breed of successful super-persons with brilliant brains and exquisite physique. Full humanity has to be seen in the likeness of the self-giving love of the crucified Christ.

d) This leads us to a further criterion. Power which reflects the power of the Christ is a power that is exercised within the community of sharing, built on communion with the Triune God. It is a power that is shared, as life within the Trinity is shared.

The question we ask here is whether all persons, as children of God, participate in the agencies of power, or whether there are groups that are excluded, for example on the basis of sex, age, handicaps, economic circumstances, social marginalization. In asking that question it should be noted that we have to think not only of sharing in decisions, but of the exercise in common of all the gifts given within a community such as, for example, healing, teaching, organizing, caring.

Any use of power that suppresses the loving exercise of gifts is an abuse that ultimately leads to the dehumanizing of persons. The clericalization of the church and the resultant withdrawal of power from the laity is a blatant expression of the abuse of power. This problem is heightened by the fact that when church structures place power in the hands of a few or even one person, a pyramidical system is created with the inherent danger of the monopolization of that power.

The Spirit's empowerment is bestowed upon the whole people of God. Therefore structures and policies should provide equality of opportunity for women and men to exercise their gifts throughout the life and leadership of the new community in Christ. In this way the ecclesial community will be a witness of a new society in which power is shared and gifts recognized as complementary.

e) In this regard, we especially deplore the lack of power exercised by women in so many churches. The Bible teaches that women are created equally in God's image and are baptised equally into the one church of Christ in whom there is neither male nor female.

f) To indicate one other criterion, the question has to be raised about the exercise of power through the dissemination of knowledge. An institution or leader exercises control over interpretation, release, and retention of knowledge. Consciously or unconsciously, the truth may be subtly distorted. Highly technical language not only excludes many from taking part in discussion of faith, but can also become an idol to be worshipped. We must ask whether what is being propagated or taught is open to the truth that is Christ, or is it instead closed idolatrously within itself as ideologies are closed.

As we have already noted, patterns of theology, too, can be evolved which are used as instruments of power and oppression, not least because such formulations cannot be used by oppressed people to express their understanding of God in Christ. The fact that different theological formulations are now being developed with accents on God's action in the liberation of the oppressed, of women, of black peoples—asks new and demanding questions of traditional theological expressions.

Money

14. The use of financial power has to be judged by these criteria. Where money comes from and how it is used within the church is an important aspect of the church's use of power. The source of money affects the ways in which it can be used. Some churches receive money from church taxes and/or from their governments. This may place limitations on its use and on the freedom of the church itself. The church can be used as a tool for political power. Voluntary contributions from some organizations and individual sources can also have a similar effect.

By what right do we assume that churches should accumulate funds to be invested? This question, we feel, requires a great deal more consideration than we have been able to give it. Even when this is accepted, the investment policy of the churches can reflect where they stand in relation to the oppressed. Where money for the work of the churches is received from rich churches or organizations, a feeling of dependency can be created and the relationship between donor and recipient affected. Money must be considered as a tool of common sharing. The economically poor have a right to play an equal part in the common sharing of the resources of earth. Church money should be used to support the struggle of the poor to end the unjust society.

Community in Christ and church structures

15. In the New Testament the church is affirmed to be the Body of Christ, a community of believers which assumes institutional form within history. In the exercise of power to fulfil its mission, the church in its members has sometimes engaged in the subtle or obvious abuse of the authority granted to it by God. It may refuse to accept new forms of communal life and mission, especially if they directly challenge such abuses.

In these cases, the community-in-mission, for example, a "comunidad de base," becomes a victim of unyielding forms or structures rather than being served by them.

Such "comunidades de base," which have in the last twenty years developed in very large numbers, particularly in Latin America, alongside the institutional churches, present the ecclesiastical institution with a challenge, particularly in relation to the structures of power within the church as they now operate. Power structures in the church are often regarded as unchangeable because they are thought to be sacred. Instead of presenting an image of a serving, sharing community, the ecclesial institution can thus reflect the structures of domination and exploitation present in society. It may then take these and reinforce them by a process of sacralization. Where this occurs it has led to a distortion between the practice of the church and its real message as Good News to the oppressed. Nevertheless each new form can be tempted itself to become in some ways a new structure of oppression if it is not constantly open to the changing needs of its members.

16. Without attempting to build a new model, we can underline some of the key features which shape these "comunidades de base" and which confront the structures of the institutional church as it looks forward to its continuing task of mission and evangelism:

—the mission of the community in Christ is to prepare itself and all people for the coming reign of God by the proclamation of the Good News;
—the structures at the service of this community must be dynamic, flowing and flexible, allowing for the creativity of all members of the community and the emergence of all kinds of ministry;
—the ongoing process of formation has to be based on the daily living experience of the people for the full realization of their humanity;
—this necessarily requires that the church be politically and socially aware of the struggles of the oppressed and involved in them;
—consequently the Word of God must be read from the point of view of the oppressed.

Repentance and restructuring in mission

17. In the light of this we must affirm that the crucified Christ not only challenges the structures of society, but also the institutional churches' structures. An effective response to this challenge is crucial to the fulfilment of the mission entrusted to the church by the risen Christ. It calls for repentance and restructuring:

Churches are tempted to be self-centred and self-preserving, but are called to be serving and sharing. Churches are tempted to be self-perpetuating, but are called to be totally committed to the promises and demands of the kingdom of God. Churches which are tempted to continue as clerical and male-dominated are called to be living communities in which all members can exercise their gifts and share the responsibilities. Churches which tend to be decaying or moribund from stifling structures are called to be living communities in which all members can exercise their gifts and share the responsibilities. Churches are tempted to be exclusivist and privileged but are called to be servants of a Lord who is the crucified Christ who claimed no privilege for himself but suffered for all. Churches tend to reflect and reinforce the dominating, exploiting structures of society but are called to be bodies which are critical of the status quo. Churches are tempted to a partial obedience but are called to a total commitment to the Christ who, before he was raised, had first to be crucified.

18. It would seem to many of us that biblically, theologically and pastorally there is no reason why women should be excluded from any position in the churches. Those who affirm this feel bound to urge upon those churches which exclude the full participation of women in top leadership that ways be sought in which women can be increasingly involved in positions of full responsibility. We have to acknowledge, however, that sharp differences of opinion have been expressed on both sides of this issue, and that no consensus can be reached in our section. We urge that the mission of the church demands a sustained exploration of this unresolved ecumenical debate. A further issue concerns the pyramidical pattern of the structure of some churches. The teaching and example of Jesus on power and leadership is that these functions must be exercised in service. The churches are called to bear wit-

ness to this. Traditionally this has been seen as affecting the style with which power is exercised. Many of us feel bound to ask whether it should not also determine the structure of authority. We report that we were unable to reach unanimity on this sensitive issue which raises difficult questions for all churches. But as the section was asked to examine church structures in the light of the crucified Christ, we cannot lightly pass over this question.

C. *In relation to evangelism*

19. Jesus charged his disciples with the mandate to announce his Gospel to the ends of the earth till his return at the end of time. "Go and make disciples of all nations teaching them to observe what I have commanded." It is important that the content and mode of evangelism be reviewed in our day in the light of the advance of biblical knowledge, of our own mistakes of the past, and the emergence of new forces and problems in the present. Jesus is the core of the Gospel. "Love one another as I have loved you" is the message of his life and "repent and believe the Good News" was his teachings. This demands a radical change of attitude on the part of all who respond.

Genuine evangelism therefore is the proclamation of Jesus as Saviour and Lord who gave his life for others and who wants us to do likewise, setting us free by declaring God's forgiveness. Evangelism is true and credible only when it is both word and deed; proclamation and witness. To say this is not to suggest that evangelism derives its power from the good deeds of Christians; our failures in obedience, however, can act as stumbling blocks.

In a world of large-scale robbery and genocide, Christian evangelism can be honest and authentic only if it stands clearly against these injustices which are diametrically opposed to the kingdom of God and looks for response in an act of faith which issues in commitment. Christian life cannot be generated, or communicated, by a compromising silence and inaction concerning the continuing exploitation of the majority of the human race by a privileged few. "You cannot love the God whom you do not see, if you do not love the neighbour whom you see" (I John 4:20). The neighbour today also is fallen among robbers as in the Gospel parable. Woe unto the evangelizer who proclaims the word but passes by this neighbour like the priest and the Levite in Jesus' parable.

The unity and integrity of social action and evangelism has been suggested to us by the proposition that to issue a political challenge to the oppressor in the name of Christ may be the only authentic way of putting to him what it means to make Jesus Christ the commanding reality in his life. We thus affirm and seek to obey the mandate to bear witness among all nations to Jesus and him crucified. We reject as heretical any proclamation of a discarnate Christ, a caricatured Jesus, who is presented as not being intimately concerned with human life and relationships. Our evangelism must be set in the context of structures for global mission.

D. In the context of mission

20. In the course of our meetings, we have been led to study the significance of the crucifixion of Jesus outside the city wall. We see this as a sign, consistent with much else in his life, that he who is the centre is constantly in movement from the centre towards the periphery, towards those who are marginalized, victims of the demonic powers, political, economic, social, cultural and even—or especially—religious. If we take this model seriously, we find that we must be with Jesus at the periphery, on the margins of society, for his priorities were clear.

Mission and evangelism must be seen in the context of the crucified Christ's words to his own people: Luke 4:18–19:

> The Spirit of the Lord is upon me because he has anointed me to preach good news to the poor, he has sent me to proclaim release to the captives, and recovering of sight to the blind, to set at liberty those who are oppressed, to proclaim the acceptable year of the Lord.

This mission and evangelism are concerned with the poor, blind, captive and oppressed and their condition which is brought on by unjust economic, political and religious structures. For many years, the churches have taken these needs seriously in their charitable work. Such charity is increasingly seen as one-sided if it implies a failure to tackle causes and structures.

21. Our study and prayer together on the theme "Christ—crucified and risen—challenges human power" has led us to see special significance in the role of the poor, the powerless and the oppressed. Might it not be that they have the clearest vision, the closest fellowship with the crucified Christ who suffers in them and with them? Might it not be that the poor and powerless have the most significant word for the rich and powerful: that Jesus must be sought on the periphery, and followed "outside the city"? That following him involves a commitment to the poor? Who but the church of the poor can preach with integrity to the poor of the world?

22. A second context of mission today is dominated by interconnected powers which form a vicious cycle.

a) The power which shapes beliefs, attitudes, culture, theology, ideas and values.

b) The organizational power, types and patterns of ministry; nature of leadership; bureaucracy; discipline; etc.

c) The remunerative power: salaries and subsidies; resources for maintenance of institutions; scholarships and similar opportunities; investments; grants of various kinds; budget allocations.

d) The punitive power—law and order: withholding or withdrawing of recognition; withdrawing of support; breaking of relationships and cutting off of finances.

These four powers and their interaction reflect the pattern of a vicious cycle, both within our societies and our churches. In this reality the church imitates the patterns of world power rather than the redeeming power of the crucified Christ.

This cycle needs to be broken if a new starting point of relationship in mission is to be established. The points at which it can and must be broken will depend upon each situation and context. Not only in the "dependent" parts of the world, but also the churches in the "dominant" parts of the world.

Once the cycle is broken a process of change is initiated which challenges all powers—this is true dying and rising in Christ.

Mission at the peripheries

23. The concept of mission being from "sending" to "receiving" countries has long been replaced by a mutuality in shared mission involving a two-way flow between the churches in the industrialized countries and the so-called Third World. We would like to point to the following:

The Christian community of the People's Republic of China reminds us of the power of the crucified Christ to sustain faith and witness apart from the structures of power on which it had long been dependent. The Christian community has long shown the correlation between self-reliance and commitment to the national struggle of the people to achieve justice. As relations increase with other churches, it will be an advantage to all to learn from the experience of the church in China in wrestling with the issues of cultural identity and authentic faith.

24. We perceive a change in the direction of mission, arising from our understanding of the Christ who is the centre and who is always in movement towards the periphery. While not in any way denying the continuing significance and necessity of a mutuality between the churches in the northern and southern hemispheres, we believe that we can discern a development whereby mission in the eighties may increasingly take place within these zones. We feel there will be increasing traffic between the churches of Asia, Africa and Latin America among whose numbers both rich and poor are counted. This development, we expect, will take the form of ever stronger initiatives from the churches of the poor and oppressed at the peripheries. Similarly among the industrialized countries, a new reciprocity, particularly one stemming from the marginalized groups, may lead to sharing at the peripheries of the richer societies. While resources may still flow from financially richer to poorer churches, and while it is not our intention to encourage isolationism, we feel that a benefit of this new reality could well be the loosening of the bond of domination and dependence that still so scandalously characterizes the relationship between many churches of the northern and southern hemispheres respectively. We must in any case work for a new world order, joining in a common confrontation with powers at the centre.

In this way we have recognized that the churches in each of the three "worlds" bear primary responsibility for mission and evangelism in their own countries and regions, that it is they who are called to assume a critical stance in the name of the crucified Christ in relation to their own structures and governments, and that it is they who exercise control over their own interest as well as over all the means used in the fullfilment of their missionary and evangelistic task.

25. Only thus can we be in solidarity with churches in other regions than our own, in the exercise of mission and the pursuit of justice legitimized as service of the crucified Christ, who challenges all human power. To build inter-church relations without challenging our own power structures, which dehumanize and betray the kingdom, is to build on sand.

We feel a sense of frustration, for much of this was clearly stated during the Salvation Today conference in Bangkok in 1973. But we confess that we have continued in our sin. We need to be converted both as individuals and as church communities toward an action that reflects the crucified Christ in the way we use our power in mutual relationships among our institutions, church and secular, and especially in our relationships with the poor, alienated and oppressed.

We challenge our member churches to review their reflection and action in the light of the crucified Christ and his kingdom, facing the international economic system in our world today.

26. In light of the above reflections *we recommend* the following:

   a) Churches should engage in a constant dialogue among themselves and with others in order to understand and identify with those who are socio-economically alienated on grounds of race, ethnicity, sex, culture and religion.

   b) Western churches have billions invested in transnational corporations and commercial banks. These investments must be turned into a resource for the mission of Christ's Church which is to stand alongside the poor and the powerless. This may mean disinvestment from such transnational corporations and banks. We commend in particular the decision of the Central Committee of the World Council of Churches in Kingston, Jamaica (1979), to reaffirm the Ecumenical Development Co-operative Society (EDCS) to make money available in soft loans to the poorest of the poor and their development projects. We recommend that the CWME urge its national members to support this new ecumenical channel for alternative investment.

c) We further urge the encouragement and support of church organizations which are attempting to call transnational corporations and banks to a corporate responsibility by avoiding investing in countries which brutally oppress their people.

d) We also urge that the Church support international bodies working for a new international economic order: United Nations, UNCTAD, etc., and the challenge to participate in a global tax.

e) That the development programmes and sub-units of the World Council of Churches—CICARWS, CCPD, UIM –URM, ECLOF, Ecumenical Sharing of Resources, etc., be interpreted and supported on all levels of the member churches of the WCC.

f) That CWME and national or regional councils of churches be called upon to take the initiative in challenging churches to implement better structures of co-operation in mission, helping them to come together for the study of new possibilities for sharing in decision-making, better approaches to mutual support, ecumenical exchange of personnel, and united witness in the light of this report. In particular they should give new consideration to the reasons that led to the proposal for a moratorium. Such reasons have lost nothing of their urgency since the Bangkok conference in 1973.

g) That churches and organizations that receive economic assistance adapt their orientations and lifestyles to the poor whom they serve.

IV. "Do this . . ."

27. Central to the worshipping life of the community of the followers of the crucified Lord is the Eucharist. In our own ways we remember the Lord's death until he comes. Here at this banquet the mystery of the kingdom takes tangible form. In that act we are brought face to face with the servant nature of the commu-

nity of the crucified—its need to be broken bread and poured-out wine. We are joined in faith with the multiplicity of Christian experience around the world, and rejoice in those saints of confessing churches whose witness is a sign of the kingdom today.

Jesus' command "Do this . . ." impels us to be faithful to the truth we have already been given. We do not need more words, but the will and the courage to act. We know that such action will lead us to conflict with the powers of this world along the way of the crucified.

28. In the midst of our conference we are aware that we live in a period when international tensions have once more become dangerously intensified, and when the fate of the world is again subjected to great-power rivalry. As we go from this conference we shall not rest silent in the face of the danger of a new world conflict. We shall not accept that the future of humanity should be determined by some of the "great," whatever may be their sense of responsibility. They are prisoners of the demonic game of competing for power. Controlled as they are by the uncertainty of maintaining themselves in power as precarious leaders, they are all the more prisoners of the incensed desire of the wealthy nations to maintain the national privileges of the rich and the powerful and to do this at any price, even the price of a possible nuclear apocalypse. As we go from here in the name of him who renounced everything for the love of all, we appeal to Christians throughout the world to open their eyes to the deadly consequences of the competition for wealth, and to raise a powerful voice for the defence of peace, remembering that peace can only be assured through a just distribution of the world's resources. National egotism is a sin whose wages can only be death, perhaps the death of the whole world. Our faith in the reign of Christ must always exclude the resigned acceptance of fatalism. Therefore we must reject and resist the counsel of despair which accepts the inevitability of war.

Christ is risen!

Come Lord Jesus.

Selected Bibliography

The following publications are of particular importance for study and understanding of the Melbourne Conference.

Special issues of the *International Review of Mission* (Geneva):

July	1978	"Edinburgh to Melbourne"
January	1979	"Australia"
April	1979	"Your Kingdom Come"
October	1979	"The Kingdom of God and Human Struggles"
January	1980	"The Kingdom and Power"
April	1980	"The Church Witnesses to the Kingdom"
July	1980	"Melbourne Conference Notes"
October	1980/	
January	1981	"Melbourne Reports and Reflections"

Arias, Mortimer. "Melbourne and Evangelism," *A Monthly Letter on Evangelism* (WCC/CWME), nos. 5, 6, 7 (1981).

Bosch, David. "Behind Melbourne and Pattaya: A Typology of Two Movements," *IAMS News Letter* (Leiden), nos. 16–17 (1980): 21–33.

———. "Evangelism: As Defined by Melbourne and Pattaya," *Reformed Ecumenical Synod Mission Bulletin* (Grand Rapids), 1, no. 2 (1981): 1-10; also in *Mission Focus* (Elkhart, Ind.), 9, no. 4 (1981): 65–74.

———. "In Search of Mission: Reflections on 'Melbourne and Pattaya,' " *Missionalia* (Pretoria), 9, no. 1 (1981): 3–18.

Castro, Emilio. "Mission Today and Tomorrow: A Conversation with Emilio Castro," *International Bulletin of Missionary Research* (Ventnor, N.J.) 5, no. 3 (1981): 108–11.

Commission on World Mission and Evangelism. *Your Kingdom Come: Mission Perspectives. Report on the World Conference on Mission and Evangelism.* Geneva: World Council of Churches, 1980.

Gort, Jerald D. *World Missionary Conference: Melbourne, May, 1980. An Historical and Missiological Interpretation.* Amsterdam: Department of Missiology, Faculty of Theology, Free University of Amsterdam, 1980.

Missiology: An International Review (Pasadena, Calif.). Special issue on Melbourne and Pattaya, 9, no. 1 (1981).

Rosin, H. "Third World Aspects of Melbourne's Vision," *Exchange* (Leiden) 10, no. 29 (September 1981): 1–7.

Verstraelen, Frans J. "After Melbourne and Pattaya: Reflections of a Participant Observer," *IAMS News Letter* (Leiden), nos. 16–17 (1980): 34–50.

Contributors

Gerald H. Anderson, director of the Overseas Ministries Study Center in Ventnor, New Jersey, and editor of the *International Bulletin of Missionary Research,* was formerly professor of church history and academic dean of Union Theological Seminary, Manila, Philippines, and president of Scarritt College, Nashville.

Emilio Castro, a Methodist pastor from Uruguay, is director of the Commission on World Mission and Evangelism of the World Council of Churches, and editor of the *International Review of Mission.*

William H. Hannah is executive secretary, Department of Evangelism and Membership, Division of Homeland Ministries, Christian Church (Disciples of Christ), Indianapolis, Indiana.

Belle Miller McMaster is director of the Office of Corporate Witness in Public Affairs, General Assembly Mission Board, Presbyterian Church in the United States, Atlanta, Georgia.

Michael Oleksa, a graduate of St. Vladimir's Orthodox Seminary in Crestwood, New York, and former lecturer at the University of Alaska and at St. Herman's Seminary in Kodiak, Alaska, is now on the faculty of Alaska Pacific University in Anchorage.

Philip Potter, a Methodist minister from Dominica in the Caribbean, has been general secretary of the World Council of Churches since 1972.

Waldron Scott, president of American Leprosy Missions, Inc., was formerly general secretary of the World Evangelical Fellowship, and international field director of the Navigators.

Eugene L. Stockwell grew up in a missionary family in Argentina and later, from 1953 to 1962, was a Methodist missionary in Uruguay. Since 1972 he has occupied his present post as associate general secretary for Overseas Ministries in the National Council of the Churches of Christ in the U.S.A.

Thomas F. Stransky, C.S.P., director of Paulist Novices, Oak Ridge, New Jersey, was president of the Paulist Fathers from 1970 to 1978. He is a member of the Joint Working Group between the World Council of Churches and the Roman Catholic Church, an official consultant to the Vatican Secretariat for Promoting Christian Unity, and a participant in the Scholars' Group sponsored by the Southern Baptist Convention and the U.S. Catholic Bishops' Ecumenical Commission.

Acronyms

EATWOT	Ecumenical Association of Third World Theologians
CCPD	Commission on the Churches' Participation in Development
CIA	Central Intelligence Agency
CICARWS	Commission on Inter-Church Aid, Refugee and World Service
CWME	Commission on World Mission and Evangelism
ECLOF	Ecumenical Church Loan Fund
ECWA	Evangelical Churches of West Africa
EDCS	Ecumenical Development Co-operative Society
EMS	Evangelical Missionary Society
GNP	Gross National Product
IMC	International Missionary Council
SIM	Sudan Interior Mission
UIM—URM	Urban Industrial Mission—Urban and Rural Mission
UNCTAD	United Nations Conference on Trade and Development
WCC	World Council of Churches